French Defense

also by C. G. Wayne

- Cocobolo
- WTexas in 2 Plays

French
Defense

... a dramatic narrative in 3 movements

by C. G. Wayne

Otter Track Press

MRose Group, LLC
Wetumpka, AL

Otter Track Press

Otter Track Press is an imprint of MRose Group, LLC. Wetumpka, Alabama. www.mrose.com

First Edition: October 2014

The characters portrayed in these narratives are fictitious. Any resemblance to actual persons living or dead is coincidental.

Wayne, Clifford Gordon.
        French Defense / by C.G. Wayne—1st ed.

Summary: A narrative in dramatic form about the haunting of a New Orleans chess player.

Library of Congress Control Number: 2014953431
ISBN: 978-0-9848229-5-9
[1. DRAMA — American 2. FICTION — Literary 3. FICTION — General.]

Acknowledgements

The roots of this work rest in a Stanford playwright workshop conducted by Amy Freed many years ago. For me it was a pivotal event. Thank you, Amy Freed, for being forgiving with your comments about my writing during the workshop. It was the first enjoyable, nonjudgemental academic writing experience I had.

I am grateful for and thank...

Aunt Ivylle and Uncle Adrian who encouraged and also tolerated my early obsession with chess...

my friends, including Petra Hofer, Bill McAnulty, Lowell Lum, and Mike Smith who traded stories with me for years while we sat on the other side of cubicle walls at work...

my friends from the University of San Francisco, Erika, my instructors, and Stephanie Reents who was my mentor

my wife and children...

my Afghan Hounds, both here and departed Montana, Markey, Jolie, Niki, and King Howl

my parents.

As always, their lives have informed my writing and my hope is that this work is a tribute to them —

Contents

Foreword

I'm watching *Midnight in Paris* again while I write this and, as always, am throughly engaged in the narrative. I watch it periodically, sometimes for a background collage of emotion, sound, and imagery. It's as close as I can or probably ever will get to being there. I enjoy the opening visuals of the streets and shops in Paris, the weather, and the music. All of these elements place me in Paris.

I have never been to Paris. I always wanted to go but never made that trip. So, I've read fiction and non-fiction set in Paris. I've read historical pieces as well as watched historical documentaries. And it remains on my list of intriguing places to be. I just want to sit at a bistro table and watch the people. I want to see Peugeots and Citröens in the street – we don't have those in the U.S. anymore.

But this film not only takes me to a place I have never been, it also tells me I can go to a time that no longer exists – the Paris of history. I can know personalities of that age. I can see Zelda Fitzgerald before she broke down. I can hear her voice and see Ernest Hemmingway as pompous. There's also Alice B. Toklas and Gertrude Stein, the godmother of that expatriate literary group. The narrative carries me into a place and time outside of my immediate reality – sitting on the sofa contemplating the relationship between narrative and the nature of reality.

The nature of reality – it seems simple enough to define. Reality is what happens to us, it's what we see, touch, and feel. Everyone knows that. Except that once when driving home from Baton Rouge, my father pointed out a blue parked car (the reason why he did escapes me now) and my mother said that it was green. They argued like that for the rest of the trip home until they finally stopped talking to each other for a while. Neither would change their positon that the car was colored the way that they saw it.

If defining reality stopped at the point of a perceived shape being a car or a dog or a bird, then the nature of reality could be a simple thing to understand. However, when we focus on the details, the physics of the experience, what we believe is real becomes less certain. So what is true? What is reliable? Is blue really green?

For literature, it is the gap between two realities, between blue cars and green cars, that offers fertile ground for exploration and creation. Effective narrative engages a listener or reader in reality that is either unique to them or trancends what they have until then accepted as immutable. We might flip that around by saying readers are engaged by narratives that present them with realities that are either unique or trancend what they have accepted as immutable.

I find myself thinking of a notable and award winning writer from Mississippi who works hard at crafting narratives that for me do not differ from my own accepted sense of reality. I've tried to read his pieces, but, honestly, I'm not that engaged by something that's from my daily life. In *Aspects of the Novel*, Forster said it's not the question of *what* happens next but

the question of mystery, the *why*, that
engages a reader's intelligence.

"The facts in a highly organized novel (like *The Egoist*)
are often of the nature of cross-correspondences
and the ideal spectator cannot expect to view them
properly until he is sitting up on the hill at the end...
Why did the queen die?"

Aspects of the Novel, E. M. Forster

In literary narrative (not just my story telling), the focus of the
reader's intellect is not on the question of
what happens next but on why does it
happen. This question of why exposes a
reader's engagement in realms which they
have not yet traversed — otherwise there
could be no why.

At this moment, Henry Darger comes to mind. Perhaps it was
using the word "realms" just now. Henry's
internal reality was not of this place,
although I've read that psychiatrists have
pronounced that he was not psychotic —
maybe suffered from Asperger's and lived
an internal existance. Apparantly he did not
halucinate. I'm not so sure about the
delusional aspect of his existance though.
But, I'm a writer and question everything
that seems certain — especially when some
authority has told me of its certainty.

When one has a psychotic break, have they lost contact with
Reality or entered a reality of their own?
That is the question *French Defense* was
written to explore — the difference between
green cars and no cars.

In *Aspects of the Novel*, Forster excluded movies from
consideration as intellectually engaging

narrative forms by comparing the "movie-public" to cave dwellers - but then in 1927 he didn't have an opportunity to see Woody Allen's *Midnight in Paris.*

C. G.
Wayne
March 29,
2014

Staging

The first two movements, *The Opening* and *Middle Game*, are set in a mythical Paul Morphy Chess Club of New Orleans.

> At one end of the stage are bistro tables and chairs with chess sets. On the back wall is a large, wall mounted, felt tournament "chess board." At the other end of the stage is the lounge area containing a stuffed armchair, floor lamp, end table, and telephone. A sign saying "Paul Morphy Chess Club of New Orleans" is draped across the wall on that side of the stage. Old chess notation is used for the description of the moves because it is more visually descriptive than contemporary algebraic notation.

The third movement, *End Game*, has three settings.

> The first setting is a French Quarter Bar named "The Black Cat Club." The *Best of Warren Zevon* is playing in a loop as backgroud music. The tables from the chess club are now used as tables in the bar. There is a small platform for an exotic dancer in the back (in place of the tournament board). The sign saying "Paul Morphy Chess Club" is replaced by a sign saying "The Black Cat Club" and there is a dim spotlight on the dancers' platform.

> The second setting is Audubon Park near the Newman Bandstand on Magazine Street. A backdrop of oaks is displayed with a park bench and a concrete railing that runs along the edge of a pavilion.

> The final setting, *Coda*, returns to the Paul Morphy Chess Club of the first two movements.

Characters

Player: Late thirties to early forties. He is a chemist who is unemployed; plays chess; is divorced; uses the French Defense to counter PK4 openings; "talks" to a ghost that he may have had an affair with years ago. In *The Opening* and *Middle Game* he is dressed in slacks and sport shirt. In the *End Game* he is dressed in a dirty T-shirt and blue jeans.

Celeste/Lisa: In her late twenties to mid thirties. She taught literature in a south Texas junior college and has a sideline of moving drugs from south Texas to New York. She is dressed in blue jeans and a T-shirt. Carries her cell phone in her hip pocket. In the bar scene from the *End Game*, she is Lisa, the exotic dancer, wearing a leopard skin bikini.

Noah Spielmann: Mid sixties, a retired teacher who joined the chess club after his wife died. Suspected by Player of being a DEA agent. Always wears a dark suit, white shirt and tie.

Dr. Winter/Bartender: Psychologist/therapist dressed neatly, professional appearance. In the bar scene from the *End Game* and the final scene of *Coda*, he is a flashy Freench Quarter bartender, dressed in a shirt unbuttoned down the chest, wearing a gold necklace.

Raymond: A young "biker" chess player - long hair and beard. He wears blue jeans, T-shirt, with leather vest or denim jacket with cut off sleeves and a bike club logo across the back. He has the standard biker wallet with long chain clipped to his belt loop.

MC: Middle aged manager of the Paul Morphy Chess Club of New Orleans. Dressed in a tux or dark suit; he is the petty and benign despot of the chess club.

<u>The Opening</u>

Scene I
Setup

MC walks to the back of the chess club and stands by the tournament board on the wall. Electronic equipment including a computer monitor and video camera are scattered around him. He's looking at it when Player walks in carrying his chess computer and chess clock.

Player: Hey, MC.

MC: Player.

Player: What'cha got back there.

Player begins setting up his chess computer and clock.

MC: A new setup for the tournament board.

Player: Yeah? What's the setup.

MC: I got a new camera setup on the main table *(points up at the ceiling)* so I can see it from back here. I've also got the tournament board *(points at the wall mounted tournament board)* tied into the internet.

Player: Cool...

MC: If it works. Mind if I post your practice while I test it?

1

French Defense — The Opening

Player: I'm just running through some variants
                 of the French. That's all.

MC: Perfect.

*Player sits at the center table facing the lounge area, his
chess computer is set up and the center spot on a chessboard
with all pieces in their initial home positions.*

*Player moves the King Pawn to King 4 and hits the top of the
chess clock to stop the timer.*

Player: Pawn to King 4.

*MC moves the corresponding pieces on the wall mounted
tournament chess board when their position is announced.
When MC is not moving pieces, he adjusts settings and
connections on the equipment around him.*

*Spielmann, dressed in a dark suit and carrying a newspaper,
walks across the stage and sits at the table by the wall.*

Spielmann: Afternoon, gents. Hey, Player. Aren't you
                 playing Raymond tonight?

Player: Tomorrow night.

Spielmann: He put a nice combination together
                 yesterday against Errol.

Player: He's still a kid.

Spielmann: But he plays well.

Player: He's a kid.

*Spielmann opens his newspaper to the chess column and
starts moving pieces on his board.*

Spielmann:	*(without looking up from his board)* My daughter called me yesterday.
Player:	*(absentmindedly)* That's good.
	Black. Pawn to King 3.

Player moves the piece on the board and hits the chess clock. MC moves the piece on the tournament chessboard.

Spielmann:	She wants me to move down there, but I don't think so.
Player:	Why don't you?
Spielmann:	What would I do down there? Sit around all day with all the other grayhairs.
Player:	See your grandkids.
Spielmann:	I don't have any.
Player:	Is she married?
	White. Pawn to Queen 4.

Player moves the piece on the board and hits the chess clock. MC moves the piece on the tournament chessboard.

Spielmann:	No. She's got a boyfriend.
	But I don't think they're going to get married.
	What about you?
Player:	*(looks up from his chess board)* What?
Spielmann:	You got any children?

Player:	*(looks back down at his chess board)* Two.
	A boy and girl. They live out in California with their mother. They're grown.
Spielmann:	Divorced?
Player:	Me? Yeah.
Spielmann:	I see. Ever think about getting married again?
Player:	Once.
Spielmann:	Really?
Player:	Last fall. I was down in Texas and met somebody.
Spielmann:	What happened?
Player:	It didn't work. That's all.
Spielmann:	What were you doing over there?
Player:	I had a contract with one of the refineries. I'm a chemist.
Spielmann:	Lots of work down there for chemists. What town, Sugarland?
Player:	*(looks up)* No, Freeport. On the coast, south of Houston.
Spielmann:	I'm not familiar with it.
Player:	I was staying out on the beach. A little town called Surfside. It was great. *(looks*

down at his chess board) But that was a
while back.

I've got to run through a few openings
for the game tomorrow.

Spielmann: I guess I better let you get back to your
board.

Player: Yeah.

*Spielmann reopens the newspaper to the chess column and
starts moving pieces on the board. The light on him dims and
our attention shifts to Celeste who walks out on the stage
with her bottle of Bushmills and a highball glass.*

The light comes up on Celeste.

Celeste: The Gulf is pretty rough today.

Player looks up at her.

Player: There's a storm coming in.

*She swats her arm and occasionally waves in front of her
face.*

Celeste: Even with this wind like it is, mosquitoes
still manage to find food.

                You from around here?

Player: No. Los Angeles.

Celeste: That's a long ways from here. What are
you doing down here in Brazoria?

Player: What's Brazoria?

Celeste:	Hon, you're standing in it. In fact, you're standin in the middle of Texas history right here. You know that?
Player:	No. I didn't.
Celeste:	Sure. See down that way? That's where Santa Anna signed over Texas.
Player:	Doesn't look like much.
Celeste:	See that dark shape out there past the surf? That's what's left of a blockade runner from the Civil War.
Player:	Not much to look at either.
Celeste:	Damn. You're a wet blanket aren't you? So why are you here?
Player:	I'm a chemist over at Phillips.
Celeste:	That sounds exciting.
Player:	Not really.
Celeste:	That was a sarcasm.
Player:	*(embarrassed)* oh.
Celeste:	Where are you staying?
Player:	*(points out at the audience)* That little motel over there.
Celeste:	Cute.

Player:	It's not bad for cinder blocks and plywood.
Celeste:	The murals are nice.
Player:	Umh. Bright. But I like it.

She sits in the chair, pours herself a drink, sips it.

Player:	You live around here?
Celeste:	I've got a place over in Lake Jackson.
	What's your name?
Player:	Player.
Celeste:	You serious?
Player:	Like a heart attack. What's yours?
Celeste:	Celeste.
Player:	Pretty name. So, what're you doing out here?
Celeste:	Walking. I like coming down here at dusk to watch the lights from the rigs.
Player:	Looks like a bunch of little towns out there.
	I was heading over to the Purple Cow to get a burger. Want to go?
Celeste:	Sure. Why not.

Player: We walked over to the Purple Cow and ate hamburgers.

Celeste: I had a quarter pounder with onion rings. And a Hieneken.

Player: They had good burgers.

Celeste: And we talked...

Player: for a couple of hours...

Celeste: bout old movies.

Player: You liked me then.

Celeste: You were fun and Jerry wasn't. He's such a maniac.

Player: Yeah, Jerry. Turned out you were married with a kid.

Celeste: You knew that up front. Didn't slow you down any.

Player: No. I guess not. He was out of town most of the time.

Celeste: And we got a little careless.

Player: That was later.

Celeste: *(she sips her drink)* Small towns see everything.

Player: That night we went back to your house...

Celeste:	after the Dragons showed up at the Cow...
Player:	and watched movies.
Celeste:	Jerry hates my old movies...
Player:	*The Third Man...*
Celeste:	It's one of those unsettling films.
Player:	A typical Orson Wells film.
Celeste:	I always think Wells should be a good guy. And I don't understand why he would sell bad penicillin.
Player:	I didn't like it.
Celeste:	They never say and it just pisses me off.
Player:	Sure they do. He was in the Black Market. That's why they were trying to arrest him.
Celeste:	That's what they said in the film. But I don't think he knew. Something else was going on. I can't believe it was just money. That's too simple.
Player:	Offhand, I can't think of any film where Wells played a really good guy.
Celeste:	He was such a kid back then. I think he liked being dangerous.
Player:	Black. Pawn to Queen 4.

French Defense — The Opening

Player moves the piece on the board and hits the chess clock.
MC moves the piece on the tournament chessboard.

                    The pressure on the center builds.

Celeste: Which opening are you using?

Player: French Defense. The classical. It's my
                    favorite against King Pawn openings.

Player is enthusiastic and animated while Celeste yawns and
sips her Bushmills.

                    What fascinates me about this defense is
                    the understated way it attacks White.

Celeste: You're nuts. You know that?

Player: Second move and bam! He has to decide.
                    I like that. It's the threat of attack not an
                    actual attack that forces white to choose
                    a course of action on the second move of
                    the game...

Celeste: God, you sound like one of those chess
                    commentaries.

Player: ...Defend the center. Advance in the
                    center...

Celeste: Sometimes I wonder why I used to think
                    you were interesting.

Player: ...Pawn exchange. Or sacrifice the king
                    pawn. White can't wait.

Celeste walks over and studies the board.

Celeste: It's not my favorite opening but I'll play
             you.

Player: I didn't know you played.

Celeste: There's more to me than you know.

Player: I bet.

Celeste: I had a 1600 rating when I was in college.

Player: That's not bad. Do you remember the
             French?

Celeste: Do you?

Player: All right then, Miss Smartass. It's the 3rd
             move. White.

Celeste: OK.

             White. Knight to Queen Bishop3.

*Celeste goes back to sit in the stuffed armchair. She never
moves the pieces or watches the board. Player moves them
for her and MC moves the corresponding piece on the wall
mounted tournament chessboard.*

             I'll stick with the standard line for
             awhile. You know they turned it into a
             radio show.

Player: What?

Celeste: *The Third Man.*

Player: How could they do that? He was killed.

Celeste: It's from the time before the time in the movie.

Player: Never heard of it.

Celeste: Orson Wells did that too. But it was called something else. *Harry Lime* or something like that.

                In that one he was just a bit shady, not evil like they made him out in that movie.

Player: But the movie came first. And he was a crook.

Celeste gets up and walks around the stage, sipping her whiskey.

Celeste: I still don't think the movie was right. I don't believe he knew the penicillin was bad.

Player: Com'on. He's only a character in a movie.

Celeste: But he wasn't a monster like they made him in the movie. Just a bit shady.

Player: Then it was a crappy film.

Celeste: *(she snaps)* It was a great film. It made you feel like you had been somewhere.

                You know they actually filmed in Vienna.

Player: You sure? It looked like a set to me.

Celeste: It was real. That was real damage from the war.

Player: I'll have to watch it again.

Celeste: It was only a few years after the war.

Celeste flops down in the chair and pours another drink.

                 Have you heard from your wife lately?

Player: Ex-wife. She got remarried. I told you
                 about that.

Celeste: Yeah. That's why I asked. I figured it'd
                 piss you off.

Player: You were always mean to me.

                 Black. Knight to King Bishop 3.

Player moves the piece on the board and hits the chess clock.
MC moves the piece on the tournament chessboard.

Celeste: Just pulling your leg, hun. Not going to
                 go for that pawn yet?

Player: Not yet. You'd just zap me with your
                 knight and then I'd have that bastard
                 sitting in the center.

Celeste: You're so suspicious. *(casually waves her*
                 hand at the board) It's such an easy target
                 out there by itself.

Player: No thanks. I'll wait a little longer before I
                 nail it.

Celeste: You're sweet.

Player: Thanks. *(he smiles)* You are too.

Celeste: White. Bishop to King Knight 5.

Player moves the piece on the board and hits the chess clock.
MC moves the piece on the tournament chessboard.

                     Still paying alimony? *(laughs)* It's so easy
                     to pull your chain.

Player: That's 'cause I've got so many of them.

                     Black. Bishop to King2.

Player moves the piece on the board and hits the chess clock.
MC moves the piece on the tournament chessboard.

                     No. Lisa got remarried to some guy last
                     year.

Celeste: Does he make good money?

Player: He's a mechanic. How's that.

Celeste: That's ok I guess. No more alimony.

Player: Or child support. The kids outgrew that.

Celeste: So you're a free man.

                     White. Pawn to King5.

Player moves the piece on the board and hits the chess clock.
MC moves the piece on the tournament chessboard.

Player: Sort of. My son's still in college. Passing
                     up the pawn?

Celeste: The tension builds. Make him pay his
                     own way.

Player: Yeah.

Celeste laughs and he looks up at her.

Player: Black. Knight to Queen2.

Player moves the piece on the board and hits the chess clock.
MC moves the piece on the tournament chessboard.

Celeste: Did you ever finish your paintings?

Player: No. I had to leave them at the motel. I
               didn't have room to pack them.

Celeste: So. What happened to you? You never
               called.

Player: *(quietly)* No, I didn't.

Celeste: I was waiting.

               White. Pawn to King Rook4.

Player moves the piece on the board and hits the chess clock.
MC moves the piece on the tournament chessboard.

Player: Damn.

Celeste: Gottcha, you bastard.

Player: Very good... very good. This is a nice
               complication.

Celeste: Why didn't you call?

Player: I told you. I didn't have a chance.

Celeste: Bullshit.

Player:	I got a contract in New York and had to leave.
Celeste:	You're so full of crap.
Player:	I had to be there by 8 Monday morning.
Celeste:	And you never called.
Player:	I think about you all the time.
Celeste:	bullshit excuse.

Celeste tucks her legs under her. Her cell phone rings and she answers it.

Hello.... Damn it. Where have you been?... Don't you bullshit me man. You were supposed to pick up Tuesday!... I got stuff in El Paso waiting on you.... Get your ass in gear or get out. And you know what that means. You hear me?...Good.

She puts the phone down, picks up the remote, aims it at the audience and turns the tv on. Sound of a tv show from off stage.

Player:	Still running?
Celeste:	Pays the bills.
Player:	What a waste.
Celeste:	Paying bills?
Player:	Smartass.
Celeste:	Still Mr. Straight-Jacket.

Player: Where's your daughter?

Celeste: At my mother-in-law's. Why?

Player: What's she going to do when the feds
                    haul your skinny ass off to jail?

Celeste: That's not going to happen. Got it
                    covered.

Player: Bullshit. They got you covered.

Celeste: *(she fakes her innocence)* I'm just a
                    schoolteacher.

Player: I forgot about that part. Guess that puts
                    you in the clear.

Celeste: Bastard.

Player: That's me.

Celeste: You can be a real bastard sometimes.

Player: You've taken this opening into an
                    interesting variation.

                    Black. Pawn to Queen Rook3.

*Player moves the piece on the board and hits the chess clock.
MC moves the piece on the tournament chessboard.*

Celeste: And *The Third Man* wasn't a Wells film.
                    Wells was just in it. Korda, Selznick, and
                    Reed produced it. Reed directed it. So it
                    was his film. Actually, Korda is the name
                    you always hear with that film.

17

Player: Excuse me. I moved Pawn to Queen Rook3.

Celeste: I heard you. And Wells didn't have that much screen time either. It's just his first scene everybody remembers.

Player: Are you going to play anymore?

Celeste: In a minute. I want to finish my drink.

Player: That's a recipe for winning chess.

Celeste: Yeah. Yeah.

                    I can't stand this show. *(she uses the remote to turn the tv off)* I keep trying to watch it but they're so goddamn pathetic. My god. They're such losers.

Player: Last week the Inquisitor said she was gay.

Celeste: You believe that crap?

Player: Just the covers.

Celeste: I don't think I've ever read one.

Player: A guy at the plant read them.

Celeste: Sure. You know I'm pretty good at spotting losers. Not so good with winners.

                    You ever go to the races?

Player: What kind?

Celeste: Horse.

Player: Sometimes.

Celeste: You know how I bet?

Player: No. How?

Celeste: I watch the horses when they come out
            on the track. You can't tell anything
            watching them in the paddock. But when
            they hit the dirt that's when you know
            which ones are losers.

Player: How's that?

Celeste: Losers lay their ears back. *(sips from her
            glass)* Scares the hell out of them when
            their hooves hit the track. Doesn't matter
            what they act like in the paddock, when
            they touch that track if those ears lay
            back you know its a loser.

Player: What about winners? They stick up their
            tails?

Celeste: Jerk. Their ears shoot forward.
            Sometimes you see them in the paddock
            with their ears back and you think this
            horse is a dog. But they get to the track
            and those ears shoot forward. They're
            psyched. You can see it. They want to
            run.

*Celeste stands up and wanders slowly around the stage
looking out at the audience like she was looking outside her
house at the backyard.*

Player: Then what?

Celeste: I mark off the ones that are going to lose.
            You're usually left with three or four
            "maybe" winners.

Celeste sips from her glass.

Player: Sounds real scientific.

Celeste: That's why I can't stand this tv show.
            After they cancel this thing you won't see
            any of these people again. Maybe baggin'
            groceries. Did you ever see that movie,
            Casey's Shadow?

Player: Never heard of it.

Celeste: Marissa hated it. I never figured out why.
            So I'd watch it just so I could watch her.
            But I never figured out what it was. She
            hated it.

Player: What's it about?

Celeste: It's a racehorse flick with Walter
            Matthau as a old coonass farmer. Sounds
            screwed up but he did ok. Not too New
            York. And there was a horse and a boy
            and they ran him at a race.

Player: The boy?

Celeste: The horse, you ass. This was quarter
            horse racing though, not thoroughbred.

Player: Yeah.

Celeste: And the horse gets hurt at the end so
            they have to work like hell to keep him

from being put down. Or maybe they
did. Put him down. I don't remember.

Player: Sounds like a tear jerker.

Celeste: Marissa hated it. I never figured out what
it was she didn't like.

She sits down across from him at the chessboard.

You can be a real bastard sometimes.
Why didn't you call me.

Player: I told you.

Celeste: You're lying.

Player: Leave me alone.

Celeste: Hell no.

Player's eyes remain on the board but he is not moving.
Celeste is watching him. Player looks up at Celeste.

Celeste: *(sneers)* You're a loser.

White. Queen to Knight 4.

Player moves the piece on the board and hits the chess clock.
MC moves the piece on the tournament chessboard.

Player: You talking about my game?

Celeste: You. You bastard. You ran away. Like
those pricks in that tv show.

Player: I'm a loser 'cause I didn't call you?

Celeste: No. Cause you ran away.

21

Player: Yeah. I know. It was a chickenshit thing to do. I took the contract in New York. But I had to be there by Monday morning.

Celeste: That's crap.

Player: Ok. (*he leans back in his chair and looks at her*) Jerry caught me going over to see you, we got into it and I shot him with that SIG.

Celeste: (*she looks at him and laughs*) I don't know what you think you did but you didn't shoot Jerry. He's making a run to New York right now. Besides if you did nobody'd care. The cops'd just figure it was some kind of busted deal and blow it off.

If you had.

Player: I did.

Celeste: You didn't. That's why nobody came after you. Moron.

Player: Sure they did.

Celeste: Who?

Player: Him. (*motions to Spielmann*)

The light comes up on Spielmann.

Celeste: That old fart? You're crazy.

Player: He doesn't really play chess. He's DEA. He just sits there everyday talking about his daughter in Florida so he can watch me.

Celeste: Oh, that convinces me.

Player: I bet he doesn't even have a daughter.

Celeste: You are crazy.

Player: He's the only one in here that doesn't talk about chess.

Celeste: What are you talking about? He's over there right now running through openings or something.

Player: Hell, Celeste, he's just moving pieces. He's not really doing anything. See that newspaper? He's running through a chess problem.

Celeste: You idiot. Why would he be watching you? For what? If DEA wanted you they'd just pick you up. They wouldn't be watching you. You see this guy any place else but here?

Player: No. But that doesn't mean they aren't out there.

Celeste: So why would they be watching you?

Player: Maybe they think I work for you.

Celeste: You're wack. You tell me you ran away because you thought you capped Jerry. And then you tell me that old man over there is DEA and he's watching you. And

all that time I'm sitting there in the dark
waiting for you to call.

You're one crazy bastard.

Player ignores her and resumes studying the board.

Player: They're after you too. I keep telling you.
You just won't listen. You have to get
out.

I'll show you.

Player suddenly gets up, walks over to Spielmann, and stands behind him.

Player: What are you doing?

Spielmann: Working on the problem from last
week's Picayune.

Player: Queen to king's bishop 4.

Spielmann: What?

Player: Queen to king's bishop 4. Mate in three
moves.

Spielmann: You're annoying.

Player: That's what they say. Actually, "You're
such a crazy bastard," is what they
usually say. (*and looks at Celeste*)

Spielmann: Are you ok?

Player: I'm peachy. Just peachy.

Player walks back to his table and sits down. Spielmann turns in his chair and watches him.

It's that damn Celeste. She always rattles me.

Celeste walks up and sits down at the table.

Celeste: So, I always rattle you?

Player: Yes, you do.

Celeste: Sounds like you really have it bad for me.

Player: Could've, but things just worked out bad. That husband of yours was a little extreme.

Celeste: He's a pistol. When we were in college he used to go out to these cowboy bars and get in fights just to fight. He was like that. He was a mad drunk.

Player: He was a mad sober.

Celeste: Bada boom. You're a regular comedian.

Player: Sorry. I didn't like him.

Celeste: Yeah, but you're not sorry.

Player: I was being polite.

Celeste: You know, when he's on crank he can drive straight through from the Rio Grande valley right up to New York City. He's just crazy.

Player:	How'd you get hooked up with that guy, anyway?
Celeste:	I don't know. He was exciting to be with, and my dad hated him.
	Everybody in town was just absolutely terrified of Jerry. He could beat the shit out of anybody. Are you going to move?
Player:	Don't rush me. This is a key move for black. King to Bishop 1 or pawn to King Bishop 4.
Celeste:	You know the thing about all of these book openings is that white always ends with the advantage. No matter what you do you get to the end of the opening and it says that white has a positional advantage. Or has a decisive advantage.
Player:	Unless white screws up.
	Black. King to Bishop1.

Player moves the piece on the board and hits the chess clock. MC moves the piece on the tournament chessboard.

Celeste:	Not likely.
Player:	What about Jerry. That was a screw up.
Celeste:	Only later.
	White. Queen to Bishop4. White secures a small positional advantage. See, I told you so.

Player moves the piece on the board and hits the chess clock.
MC moves the piece on the tournament chessboard.

Player: The game ain't over yet. Remember *The Big Chill*?

Celeste: Of course. I like to play it in the winter when it's raining. What made you think about it?

Player: All your drug running crap. First time I saw it I was so pissed William Hurt was playing a small time runner. I always liked him. And this guy he was playing was such a loser.

Celeste: I didn't think he was a loser.

Player: Sure he was. He had a broken down Porsche. No job except doing small time drug deals.

Celeste: So? That doesn't make him a loser.

Player: What movie were you watching?

Celeste: A loser is somebody that can't cope. They live all screwed up. Like that damn tv show. But he was out there. He was doing.

Player: Get real. You're saying he was coping because he was driving around with a box of speed strapped to the bottom of a wrecked out Porsche.

Celeste: I'm saying he was doing. He wasn't a passenger. He was a driver. He was looking for something.

Player: Bull. Shit. He wasn't driving anything. He was drifting. That was the point of the whole goddamn movie. A bunch of drifting yuppies.

Celeste: No way. The only reason he was there was because he was searching.

Player: For god's sake, he was there for a funeral.

Celeste: Just because he wasn't materially successful...

Player: Materially successful? If it wasn't for Glenn Close...

Celeste: She was so good.

Player: ...smiling at the end you wouldn't even think he might pull it out.

Celeste: That's why it was such a good movie.

They stop talking and glare at each other.

Player: She and William Hurt were about the only interesting characters in that film.

Celeste: Most people aren't interesting, really. But they all believe they are.

Player: I never bought the happy smiley way she turned her husband over to get whats-her-name pregnant. I can just hear Lisa telling me its ok to go screw some friend of hers so she could have a baby.

Celeste: It wasn't like that.

Player:	Duh. That's what *I* was seeing.
Celeste:	Men.
Player:	What's that go to do with it?
Celeste:	When I watch it now I think Jo Beth's husband may have been the only honest one of the bunch.
Player:	I thought he was a jerk.
Celeste:	Maybe. At the time he seemed like a jerk. But now I've started to change my mind. I think he was an inside joke.
Player:	I never think about him.
Celeste:	That scene when he's downstairs at night in the kitchen talking to the others...
Player:	I don't remember it.
Celeste:	...basically he tells them they're shallow.
Player:	Yeah? That's what critics say about the whole movie.
Celeste:	That's 'cause they don't understand it.
Player:	They don't get paid to understand.
Celeste:	They liked *Traffic*.
Player:	That's the grunge factor. Grunge makes a wading pool look deep.
Celeste:	I didn't get the whole Federale thing. The Federales I know aren't like that.

Player: Maybe it's the music.

Celeste: What do you mean?

Player: If the music was rap or maybe ICP...

Celeste: ICP? Never heard of it.

Player: Insane Clown Posse.

Celeste: What the hell is that?

Player: Some kind of violent metal rap group.
               My son liked them. He said he's a... hell I
               can't remember what the groupies call
               themselves. It's something strange.

Celeste: That's another word you don't hear
               anymore. First yuppies and now
               groupies.

Player: I'm a old guy now. So I think it'd be good
               if they laid down an ICP track over all
               those old tunes.

Celeste: That'd be weird. I wonder what it would
               look like if the music was changed to
               that.

Player: Edgy. Imagine that dancing scene in the
               kitchen.

Celeste: Freaky. I wouldn't like it.

Player: But movie critics would.
               Jeff Goldblum was good.

Celeste: I never like him in movies. He's such a
               con.

Player:	He's supposed to be.
Celeste:	I still don't like him. He looks dangerous in a crooked politician kind of way.
Player:	Hey, he'd be good as a politician wouldn't he?
Celeste:	Maybe. You know, I like the music the way it is. It's naive. That's what it's supposed to be.
Player:	Like American Graffiti?
Celeste:	I never saw *American Graffiti*.
Player:	Me either. None of it made sense to me. I grew up in Mississippi not California.
Celeste:	Oh my god!
Player:	Yeah.
Celeste:	Mississippi Burning.
Player:	I don't watch movies about Mississippi.
Celeste:	Where did you live?
Player:	A couple of places. Clinton. Just west of Jackson. But in the country mostly.
Celeste:	That doesn't tell me anything. Most of that state's in the country.
Player:	*(defensively)* Back then, maybe. There's more people now. Like everywhere else,

the country's disappearing. Like everywhere.

Celeste: Fort Worth is like that.

Player: You from Ft. Worth?

Celeste: Yeah.

Player: I drove through there once.

Celeste: We lived on the west side. Out by the base. Back then it was just open prairie. One small little clump of cheap houses.

White Settlement. Not much of a town back then. It's just one stretch of houses now.

Player: Are the houses are still cheap?

Celeste: Oh god, yes. When they shut the base down a few years ago that part of town just about died. 'Course the people are still there. Everybody was stuck out there just trying to hang on.

Player: You ever go back?

Celeste: Not often. It's sort of depressing.

Player: Yeah. Going back usually is.

Black. Pawn to Queen Bishop4.

Player moves the piece on the board and hits the chess clock. MC moves the piece on the tournament chessboard.

Celeste:	My mom still lives in the same crappy little house.
Player:	What about your dad?
Celeste:	He's passed.
Player:	Oh. What was it?
Celeste:	Heart attack. Working on the line at Generous Dynamics. They were working 3 shifts and mandatory overtime. F-16s were flying out of there every day back then. My dad worked on almost all of them. I was in school when it happened.
Player:	What'd he do?
Celeste:	He....
	I don't have any idea. He never talked about it. He just worked on the line. I never asked. Shit. It was just stuff he did.
Player:	My dad...
Celeste:	I went to UT Austin. Got a degree in literature and never went back.
Player:	My...
Celeste:	Sometimes when I fly into DFW I get a car and drive out that way. But I never stop. Just drive by to see if she's still living in that crappy little house.
Player:	Don't you ever see your mom?

Celeste:	No. When I left for Austin that was it for me. I swore I was never going back. And I never did.
Player:	Damn. You're a hardass.
Celeste:	She's just a drunk old bitch. Her and GD killed him.
	White. Pawn takes pawn.

Player moves the piece on the board and hits the chess clock. MC moves the piece on the tournament chessboard.

Celeste goes back over to the sofa and sips from her drink.

Player:	You loved your dad?
Celeste:	Sure, I guess. He was ok. She was a bitch though.
	Slept around all the time. While he was working, she was down at the Captains Den.
Player:	What's that.
Celeste:	A bar, stupid. What else would it be.
Player:	Hell, with a name like that it could have been anything.
Celeste:	It was over by the plant. Drinking everything away.
	We didn't have shit. And she stayed drunk. I don't know why he put up with it.

Player: It's hard to figure out why people do
                 what they do.

Spielmann watches him carefully, no longer paying
attention to his own chessboard.

Spielmann: You ok?

Player: Perfect. Why?

Celeste: Because you're wack, hon. If you weren't,
                 I wouldn't be sitting here talking to you.

Spielmann: I just wondered what opening you're
                 working on there? You look intense.

Player: French Defense.

Spielmann: I've never played the French. I prefer the
                 Two Knights.

Player: I'm going to use it tomorrow when I play
                 the kid. If I get black.

Celeste remains seated in the chair, drinking. Occasionally
she monitors the conversation between Player and
Spielmann.

Spielmann: He likes the Fisher openings. Is the
                 French any good against that?

Player: I like it. It puts the pressure on the center
                 right at the start. He's young. He might
                 make a mistake in the opening if he's not
                 careful.

Celeste: Losers.

Player ignores her and continues talking to Spielmann.

French Defense — The Opening

Player:	Have you played him yet?
Spielmann:	No. I signed up late for the Round Robin.
Celeste:	You need to get out of this cave.
Player:	You going to use the Two Knights?
Spielmann:	It's my favorite. I feel it lets me be more flexible.
Celeste:	...afraid to call.
Player:	What if you draw white.
Spielmann:	Carro-Kahn. What about you?
Celeste:	...chickenshit.
Player:	Nimzo-Indian. I've never had much luck with it. But I like the name. Nimzo-Indian.
Spielmann:	Why would you use an opening you don't win with?
Player:	I like the name.

Spielmann shakes his head and turns back to his board to continue his study. Player turns back to Celeste.

Player:	So a loser is somebody that plays chess in their spare time. But a small time drug dealer is doing something, so they aren't. What a load of crap.

Celeste:	What I see here is a bunch of losers hiding up in a room imagining grand strategies...
Player:	Moving drugs...
Celeste:	that don't amount to jack shit. Never getting out of this room.
Player:	Driving all night on a freeway
Celeste:	Not talking to other people....
Player:	across the country, watching for cops...
Celeste:	Memorizing games played 60 years ago...
Player:	...waiting for cops to break down the door and haul your ass to jail.
Celeste:	loser...
Player:	Take everything you have...
Celeste:	Bullshit.
Player:	Black. Knight to Queen Bishop 3.

Player moves the piece on the board and hits the chess clock. MC moves the piece on the tournament chessboard.

Celeste:	White. Knight to Bishop 3.

Player moves the piece on the board and hits the chess clock. MC moves the piece on the tournament chessboard.

You really think he's DEA?

Player: No. I just said that to piss you off. What
do you think?

Black. Queen to Bishop2.

Player moves the piece on the board and hits the chess clock.
MC moves the piece on the tournament chessboard.

Celeste: Passing up the bishop pawn?

Player: Black strengthens its position for the
coming Armageddon.

Celeste: You're so phoney.

White. Pawn to Queen Knight4.

Player moves the piece on the board and hits the chess clock.
MC moves the piece on the tournament chessboard.

The speed and intensity of the moves picks up.

White prepares.

Player: Black. Knight2 takes King Pawn.

Player moves the piece on the board and hits the chess clock.
MC moves the piece on the tournament chessboard.

The blitzkrieg begins.

Celeste: White. Bishop takes Bishop. Check.

Player moves the piece on the board and hits the chess clock.
MC moves the piece on the tournament chessboard.

Squirm you bastard.

Player: Black. King takes Bishop.

Player moves the piece on the board and hits the chess clock.
MC moves the piece on the tournament chessboard.

                 Black refuses to quit.

Celeste: White. Knight takes Knight.

Player moves the piece on the board and hits the chess clock.
MC moves the piece on the tournament chessboard.

                 It's only a matter of time before you're
                 finished. Give it up Player.

Player: Black. Queen takes Knight.

Player moves the piece on the board and hits the chess clock.
MC moves the piece on the tournament chessboard.

                 Check. I never quit.

Celeste: White. Queen takes Queen.

Player moves the piece on the board and hits the chess clock.
MC moves the piece on the tournament chessboard.

Player: Black. Knight takes Queen.

Player moves the piece on the board and hits the chess clock.
MC moves the piece on the tournament chessboard.

                 The ladies are off the board.

Celeste: White. Knight to Queen Rook4.

Player moves the piece on the board and hits the chess clock.
MC moves the piece on the tournament chessboard.

With advantage for white. That's how it always ends.

Lights dim to black.

Scene II
Round Robin

Spielmann is sitting at his table studying his chess board. MC is sitting in the armchair reading a chess book, drinking a cup of coffee and eating a beignet. Raymond walks in carrying his bag and sits at the center table.

Raymond: You seen Player today?

Raymond takes his chess set out of his bag and begins setting his pieces up. MC looks up from his reading.

MC: He was here earlier.

Raymond: We're supposed to play today.

Spielmann: He said it was tomorrow.

Raymond: He must've forgot what day it is. Again.

MC goes back to reading.

Spielmann: You known him long?

Raymond: A few months.

Spielmann: Has he always been like this?

Raymond: You mean a freak?

Spielmann: That's kind of strong.

Raymond: Yeah, he's a freak.

Spielmann: The other day he said he was a chemist.

Raymond:	*(shrugs)* Beats me. I don't know him. I just play chess against him. He's not bad when he's got it together. You a cop?

Raymond takes out his notebook and chess clock.

Spielmann:	Me? No. Why?
Raymond:	You dress like one.
Spielmann:	I'm just retired. I never got comfortable dressing in blue jeans like you young people. Not that there's anything wrong with it.
Raymond:	What's with the questions about schizo.
Spielmann:	Player?
Raymond:	Yeah. The freak.
Spielmann:	Nothing. Just curious. I see him in here working on openings.

Raymond turns his attention to his chess board. As he talks through the remaining dialog he moves pieces every 10 seconds, alternating white and black moves, tapping the clock at the end of each move just as he would in a speed chess match. Spielmann watches him practice as they talk.

Raymond:	Mostly he plays that computer. You hear him talk to it yet?
Spielmann:	This afternoon. He was calling it Celeste.
Raymond:	What a freak. They're going to lock him up before long.
Spielmann:	Is he dangerous?

Raymond: Not yet. Creepy but harmless. So how long you been a member?

Spielmann: I joined a couple of weeks ago. My wife died last year so I thought this would be something good to do. Keep my brain working.

Raymond: That's what they say. Sorry to hear about your wife. Cancer?

Spielmann: Car wreck.

Raymond: Damn. Any kids?

Spielmann: I have a daughter. But she lives in Pensacola.

Raymond: I've been to Pensacola. They had a tournament there a month ago.

Spielmann: How'd you do?

Raymond: I got slaughtered. I was just starting the tournament gig and was too nervous. I lost a wad on that one.

Spielmann: You play well.

Raymond: Thanks. I've tried to learn everything I can from Bobby Fisher.

Spielmann: Player says you like to use his opening.

Raymond: You have to master one to win. Might as well follow the Master.

Spielmann: So what do you do?

French Defense — The Opening

Raymond: I play chess.

Spielmann: I meant for a living.

Raymond: That's what I do.

Spielmann: You're kidding.

Raymond: No. I do ok. There's a few places around
              where we play for cash.

Spielmann: You mean gambling?

Raymond: Hell no. This is chess not poker. More
              like private tournaments.

Spielmann: Sounds like gambling to me.

Raymond: It's all entry fee. You put your fee in the
              pot and the winner takes the pot.

Spielmann: How much is the fee?

Raymond: It depends. Why're you so interested?

Spielmann: I never heard of people playing chess for
              money before. I always thought it was
              just like in here with guys playing for fun.

Raymond: Nobody in here plays for fun. What gave
              you that idea?

Spielmann: Oh. I just thought...
              How long does it take to play one of these
              tournaments?

Raymond: Not long. It's speed chess. 30 seconds a
              move.

Spielmann:	That's fast.
Raymond:	Fast to screw up, too.
Spielmann:	This Player, is he any good?
Raymond:	Like I said, when he's not crazy he does ok. You said he was talking to his computer today?
Spielmann:	He was calling it Celeste.
Raymond:	He probably won't be any good tomorrow then.
Spielmann:	Does he play in these tournaments?
Raymond:	Not that I know of. He's too weird. Nobody would want him in.
Spielmann:	How much do you make doing this?
Raymond:	More than playing pool over at Elmo's.
Spielmann:	I had no idea.
Raymond:	It's not Chess Federation so don't go talking about it around the club.
Spielmann:	I won't.
Raymond:	I probably shouldn't have said anything.
Spielmann:	No, no. I won't say anything. I just had no idea.

Spielmann watches him and then begins working on his own chess problem from the newspaper. He is very slow and a striking contrast to the rapid moves that Raymond makes.

French Defense – The Opening

Spielmann:	How do you do that?
Raymond:	Which part?
Spielmann:	Move so fast.
Raymond:	You have to know what you're doing.
Spielmann:	Practice I guess.
Raymond:	No. You have to know what you want and then you have to know how to get it. That's why you study the Master.
Spielmann:	I see. So you only know the one opening.

Raymond stops moving pieces.

Raymond:	I *study* one opening. That's a different thing.
Spielmann:	You don't look like a chess player.
Raymond:	Shutup. I'm practicing.

Spielmann, offended, goes back to his chess board for a couple of beats while Raymond resumes practice, then picks up his paper and leaves. Raymond turns around to talk to MC.

Raymond:	That old guy's a piece of work.
MC:	I think he's bored.
Raymond:	He looks like a cop.
MC:	You think?

Raymond:	Acts like one too. All those questions.
MC:	So why'd you tell him about the tournaments?
Raymond:	To watch his face.
MC:	How'd you do this weekend?
Raymond:	Pretty good. I picked up 5.
MC:	That'll pay your rent. Who'd you play?
Raymond:	A couple of guys up in Covington.
MC:	Who was it.
Raymond:	One's a big shot oil man up there that likes to think he's a player.
MC:	Paul Richard?
Raymond:	That's him. Lately he's been good for a match once a month.
MC:	He beat you yet?
Raymond:	I let him win enough to keep trying.
MC:	What's your rating now?
Raymond:	It's only 1850. I need to play more rated tournaments. But I got stuff to do for the bike club.
MC:	I don't understand why you're still in that.

Raymond:	They're my brothers. I couldn't let 'em down.
MC:	What is it you do anyway?
Raymond:	Stuff.
MC:	Is it legal?
Raymond:	*(looks around the room)* Do you hear a cricket in here?
MC:	Com'on, Raymond.
Raymond:	Gee Jiminy.
MC:	Ok, ok. Forget it.
Raymond:	Want a drink?

Raymond pulls out a hip flask and holds it up to MC. MC looks around the room.

MC:	Sure. I'll get us some glasses.

MC leaves and returns with two highball glasses. Raymond pours a finger of whiskey in each.

MC:	What else do you do besides this and the bike club?
Raymond:	Nothing. That keeps me busy enough. What about you?
MC:	I've got some bird dogs. And a sail boat. My wife hates the boat though. She hates the dogs too for that matter. I don't take my boat out much anymore.

Raymond:	Because of her?
MC:	It's more complicated than that. It's just not as easy anymore getting down there and taking it out. I guess I ought to sell it.
Raymond:	Maybe. Maybe you ought to take it out more. You got it in a marina?
MC:	Over by Lakefront.
Raymond:	If I was you I'd start taking it out. Sail boats are cool things, man. How'd you get this gig?
MC:	A friend of mine from college was a member. We used to play chess back then.

Anyway, a few years back when the club manager died he called me. Things were tight for me at the time so I took it. |
MC:	Which one is he?
Raymond:	You wouldn't know him. He moved to South Carolina a few years back.
Raymond:	When'd you start?
MC:	Back in '82.
Raymond:	Damn. I wasn't even born yet.
MC:	Time goes by fast.
Raymond:	Does it pay good?

MC: It's ok. I can buy beans and rice.

Raymond: You ought to play some of these
                   matches. You could make some good
                   money.

MC: That's ok. I'm not that good anymore.
                   And hunting season's coming up in
                   another month.

Raymond: What do you hunt?

MC: Quail. I got a lease on some land up
                   north of the lake. I go up there with my
                   dogs.

Raymond: You any good?

MC: We do ok. I got one dog that's really
                   good.

Raymond: How about you? Are you a good shot?

MC: Pretty good. But I don't kill very many.
                   Mainly I just watch the dogs work. It's
                   what they were born for, you know.

Raymond: I guess. We never had any dogs.

MC: Where're you from?

Raymond: Houston. Actually I was born down
                   south of there. A little town called Klute.
                   It's right on the edge of Lake Jackson. My
                   dad worked the refineries down there.

MC: What's he do?

Raymond:	Nothing now. He was a pipefitter. But he got hurt when I was a kid. Can't work anymore. Fell off a scaffold and broke his hip so he can't walk good.
MC:	That's got to be tough.
Raymond:	Yeah. It hurts him most of the time.
MC:	What's he do now?
Raymond:	Nothing. Just sits around watching tv and drinking beer, when he can get it. He's a fat old bastard now. When I was a kid, though, before he got hurt, he was strong. One time he picked up the front of a neighbors VW on a bet. He was strong. But now he just watches tv.
MC:	You know, they've got a rated tournament coming up next month in Atlanta. I think you ought to sign up.
Raymond:	I don't know.
MC:	Think about it. I'd like somebody from the club to play. You're about the best we got.
Raymond:	What day?
MC:	It's three days. The 12th, 13th, and 14th. It's a good chance to boost your rating.
Raymond:	Maybe. I'll have to check with Jim.

MC: Who's Jim?

Raymond: I work with him at the club.
               You got any kids?

MC: A boy. He's going to college up in
               Hammond.

Raymond: Smart kid?

MC: He does ok.

Raymond: What's he studying?

MC: Agriculture.

Raymond: You can study that in college?

MC: Yeah. He says he wants to be a farmer.

Raymond: Damn. I guess I thought farmers just
               went out and planted shit. I didn't know
               they had to go to college.

MC: I was hoping he'd go into computer
               science or something. I don't know
               where he came up with the agriculture
               idea.

Raymond: You ever live on a farm?

MC: Hell no. We live in Metairie.

Raymond: Man that's weird.

MC: I thought so too. But I couldn't get him
               to change.

Raymond:	How old is he?
MC:	He's 21. He'll graduate in the spring.
Raymond:	What's he going to do then?
MC:	I don't know. He hasn't figured that part out yet.
Raymond:	Good luck. Times are hard out there right now. We got a guy in the club that just lost his shop, business was so bad. And that's bikes, man. You know, those are some dedicated dudes, and for those guys to stop buying stuff for their bikes, you know times have got to be hard, man.
MC:	What do people in your club do for a living? *(smiles)* Besides play chess.
Raymond:	All kinds of things. Hey, we even got one guy that's a dentist. But mostly they do mechanic work. And welding. George has his own truck and he does contract work for the plants out there in Norco.
MC:	I guess he does pretty well.
Raymond:	Yeah. Between the club and his welding he makes a good living.
MC:	Why'd you join that outfit anyway?
Raymond:	I told you. They're my friends, man.
MC:	How long have you been in it?
Raymond:	Damn. You're as bad as that old dude.

MC: Just curious. I never knew anybody in a biker club before.

Raymond: Ok. Least I know you're no cop.

MC: No. I'm just an old chess club manager. Right up there with janitor.

Raymond: You're no janitor.

MC: I don't know. I do my share of cleaning up around here.

Raymond: Yeah, but you don't do janitor work. You don't even want to say you're a janitor. Even joking around. That's some hard work, man, and you don't get paid crap for it either.

MC: Sounds like you've done it before.

Raymond: For three months once. Right after dad fell. Nights you go in after all the people have gone home and dump their trash, vacuum their carpets, mop and wax their floors. It's no fun. And they always complain you didn't clean good enough.

                    But cleaning the johns was the worst.

MC: I can imagine.

Raymond: I dropped out of high school after that and got me a job helping out at a motorcycle shop. It paid better than fast food and I didn't have to work nights.

MC: That's when you joined the bike club?

Raymond:	After I got my bike. That was a couple of months later. Guy had a wrecked hog and I was able to get that. Scrounged some parts and got it running again. Worked out pretty good for me. Still got it. Been all over hell'n gone with that bike.
MC:	You ever finish high school?
Raymond:	Hell no. Didn't need it. I do better than any of them bastards as it is.
MC:	Which bastards.
Raymond:	The suits. Didn't seem to be much point in it.
MC:	It's not about money.
Raymond:	I hear that a lot. But it's always from folks that got money.
MC:	I don't have money.
Raymond:	You worry about how you're going to eat tonight?
MC:	No, but that's not having money.
Raymond:	When you can't buy groceries cause you got empty pockets that's not having money. You have money. You just don't pay any attention to it.
MC:	Well, that's got nothing to do with your education.

Raymond: I got a education. Just not from any schoolroom.

MC: Ok. This isn't going anywhere. You've already argued this before.

Raymond: I hear it all the time.

MC: If you ever change your mind let me know. The club has a scholarship fund you would qualify for.

Raymond: What would I need a scholarship for?

MC: To help out with your tuition and books. College isn't free you know.

Raymond: College? What about high school?

MC: That's a test you take. You want to really learn something? You want to go to college. Let me know if you change your mind.

Raymond: They wouldn't let me in.

MC: Sure they will. You're too smart to waste.

Raymond: Now, you're gettin close to pissing me off.

MC: Learning's for your brain. Money's something that happens for your stomach.

Raymond: Yeah, yeah.

MC stands up.

MC: Want me to take that glass?

Raymond: Sure. I'm done.

Raymond hands him the glass and MC leaves the stage with them. Raymond packs up his clock and chess board. MC comes back on stage.

MC: Leaving?

Raymond: Yeah. We were supposed to play, but Player got screwed up on the day. Might as well get on back.

MC: Let me know about that tournament.

Raymond: Sure. I'll check with Jim tonight. See you tomorrow.

MC: Right.

MC watches him leave then walks to the armchair and sits. The lights dim.

– French Defense –

Scene III
Tin Top

The stage is empty. Spotlight on the center chess table and on the armchair. Player walks out to the chess table, sits down, and starts setting up his board and clock. Celeste walks in carrying her bottle of Bushmills and glass, sits in the armchair, and drinks from the whiskey glass.

Celeste: I was born in Tin Top, you know.

Player: What's that.

Celeste: A little town out west of Fort Worth. On the Brazos. Up there, there's not much to the Brazos.

Player: I was born in...

Celeste: My daddy tried to farm but it didn't pan out for him. When I was three we moved to Ft. Worth.

Player: Natchez, Mississippi. My dad...

Celeste: Got a job working for General Dynamics.

Player: ...was a lawyer.

Celeste: Bucked rivets on the line.

Player: Was a partner in one of the oldest firms in Mississippi.

Dr. Winter walks in carrying a notepad and a straight-backed armless wooden chair; puts the chair by the Celeste and sits in it facing her; notepad open.

French Defense — The Opening

Player: You never let me talk.

Dr. Winter: What's that mean?

Celeste: I don't know. It's just something he used
                 to say after he was a foreman. "I started
                 out bucking rivets..." You know how
                 parents are.

Player: Who the hell is this guy?

Celeste: This is Dr. Winter. My therapist.

Dr. Winter: How did that make you feel?

Player: Shit. Why the hell did you bring a
                 shrink?

Celeste: He's a therapist.

Dr. Winter: Did it make you angry?

Celeste: Why should it. I don't care. Didn't care.
                 It was just something he used to say. He
                 was proud of it. You know?

Dr. Winter: What else did he say?

Celeste: Nothing really. He was always tired. He
                 worked two shifts when times were good.
                 And when the contracts ended he got
                 laid off and had to work two jobs. He was
                 always tired.

Player: Shrinks are a pain in the ass.

Dr. Winter turns to face Player.

60

Dr. Winter: Do I threaten you?

Player: You're just a different kind of lawyer.

Dr. Winter turns back to Celeste.

Dr. Winter: Ignore him. When he's ready to accept
                 help he'll tell us. Until then he will reject
                 anything you do to help him.

*Raymond and MC walk in. MC goes over to the wall mounted
felt tournament chess board and electronics equipment.
Raymond walks up to the table where Player is sitting.*

Raymond: Hey. Where were you yesterday?

Raymond sits down.

Player: What do you mean? I was here and then
                 I went home.

Raymond: We were supposed to play at 4.

Player: No. That's today.

Raymond: What day is it?

Player: Tuesday.

Raymond: Yesterday was Tuesday, freako. This is
                 Wednesday.

*Player stares at him for a minute, blinking, confused, and not
talking.*

Player: Guess I got the days messed up.

Raymond: What is it you do for a living anyway?

French Defense – The Opening

Player: I'm a chemist. Why?

Raymond: Just wondered. Seems like you get
messed up a lot on what day it is.
(sarcastically) That's a little different
from most people.

Player: I've been working nights.

*Player picks up a white and a black chess piece, puts them
behind his back a moment, and then holds them out.
Raymond chooses a hand - it's the black piece.*

Dr. Winter: Sometimes patience is our only ally.

*Player moves the white Pawn to King 4 and hits the chess
clock. MC makes the corresponding move on the tournament
board.*

Celeste: So. You're Bobby Fisher today.

Player: Don't piss me off. I have to beat this kid
to move up the ladder.

*Raymond moves the black Pawn to King 3 and hits the chess
clock. MC makes the corresponding move on the tournament
board.*

Celeste: Pawn to King 3. He's going for the
French.

Player: Damn. He's using my line.

Celeste: Serves you right. You're so arrogant.

Player: Not me. I'm humble. Nobody's more
humble than me. He's the one that's
arrogant.
Pawn to Queen 4.

Player moves white Pawn to Queen 4 and hits the chess clock. MC makes the move on the tournament board.

Raymond quickly matches Player by moving black Pawn to Queen 4 and hits the chess clock. MC makes the move on the tournament board.

Celeste: There it is. Pawn to Queen 4. What are you going to do.

Spielmann walks in, sits at the table next to them and quietly watches the game.

Player: I could use the Nimzowitsch. I don't think I want to go with a classical line. He's probably been studying that.

Celeste: You over analyze everything.

Player: I'll go with the Tarrasch. Knight to Queen2.

Player moves white Knight to Queen2 and hits the chess clock. MC makes the move on the tournament board.

Celeste: I don't remember this one.

Dr. Winter: I always enjoy playing chess. Of course I haven't played in years.

Raymond moves black Knight to King Bishop3 and hits the chess clock. MC makes the move on the tournament board.

Player: Knight to King Bishop3. He didn't think long about that move. I wonder if he's been studying this variation.

Celeste: You're overthinking again.

Player:	*(annoyed)* This is a game about thinking. You can't win if you don't think.
	It's time to squeeze him a bit. Pawn to King5.

Player moves white Pawn to King5 and hits the chess clock. MC makes the move on the tournament board.

Dr. Winter:	I've never been able to capitalize on the pawn to King 5.
Player:	It's the only logical development to me. The weakness of the French for black is the loss of space.
Dr. Winter:	The problem I run into when I squeeze black is that I reach a point where I can't compress the space anymore.
Celeste:	*(looks at Dr. Winter)* You're both pathetic.
Player:	If you take away black's room to develop, the game is done.

Raymond moves black King Knight to Queen2 and hits the chess clock. MC makes the move on the tournament board.

Celeste:	King Knight to Queen 2. I'd rather be grooming my dogs than sit through this.
Player:	Those aren't dogs. Those're fashion statements. Bishop to Queen 3.

Player moves white Bishop to Queen 3 and hits the chess clock. MC makes the move on the tournament board.

Dr. Winter:	What kind of dogs do you have?
Celeste:	Afghan Hounds.
Dr. Winter:	Aren't they stupid? I heard they were stupid.
Player:	Yeah.
Celeste:	That's bullshit.
Player:	They steal food right off the table.
Celeste:	You ever caught 'em? Pawn to Queen Bishop 4.

Raymond moves black Pawn to Queen Bishop 4 and hits the chess clock. MC makes the move on the tournament board.

Player:	That's not smart. That's just sneaky.
Celeste:	Did you ever catch 'em? You're just mad 'cause they only stole your food.
Dr. Winter:	*(to Player)* Do you like dogs?
Player:	Not hers. Pawn to Queen Bishop3.

Player moves the white Pawn to Queen Bishop3 and hits the chess clock. MC moves the piece on the tournament board.

	They're big, hairy, and too much work.
Celeste:	Bullshit.
Dr. Winter:	Why is this dog issue so important to you?
Player:	Me?

Celeste:	It's not my issue. But if you don't like my dogs...
Player:	Her dogs. They live in the house. You ever see a pack of Afghan Hounds in a living room? And they don't like men.
Celeste:	They just weren't too crazy about you's all.
Player:	I never saw any men they liked.
Celeste:	Knight to Queen Bishop 3. You weren't around long enough to find out.

Raymond moves black Knight to Queen Bishop 3 and hits the chess clock. MC moves the piece on the tournament board.

Player:	Knight to King 2.

Player moves the white Knight to King 2 and hits the chess clock. MC moves the piece on the tournament board.

> You're right. *(studying the board)* Maybe they'd have stopped growling at me in a couple of years.

Raymond moves the black Queen to Knight 3 and hits the chess clock. MC moves the piece on the tournament board.

Dr. Winter:	Queen to Knight 3. The Queen is loose. Always adds danger to the board.
Player:	*(annoyed)* I can't concentrate with all this talking going on.

Player studies the board. His hands move over the pieces a couple of times as if to move them but he stops before touching them.

Why don't you and your shrink go back
to where you came from and talk about
your mother or something.

Celeste: Hey, that's not nice. Why don't you talk
about yours?

Player: Nothing to talk about there. She's a living
saint.

Celeste: Your daughter then. At least *my*
daughter loves me.

Player: Yeah. That's true.

Player stares at the board.

Then they grow up and we get old.

Celeste: *(sarcastically)* That's so sad.

Player: Yeah, yeah. It is. It's all sad.

*Player stands and walks over to Celeste. Takes a sip from her
glass of Bushmills.*

Dr. Winter: *(motions at the chess board)* Are you
going to play?

Player: I don't know. I lost my train of thought.
You guys are messing me up.

Dr. Winter: We're not messing you up. You're
messing you up.

Player: I'm friggin out of my mind listening to
you guys.

Celeste: You've always been out of your mind.

French Defense – The Opening

Player:	Right.

Player remains standing while he studies the board, reaches over, moves white Knight to King Bishop 3 and hits the chess clock. MC moves the piece on the tournament board.

Raymond moves black, Pawn takes Pawn, and hits the chess clock. MC moves the piece on the tournament board.

Player sits on the arm of Celeste's chair and sips from Celeste's glass.

Celeste:	*(to DR. Winter)* He *is* nuts you know. He thinks he killed my husband.
Player:	I did. He ran me off the road down by Oyster Bayou.
Celeste:	He says he shot him.
Player:	Jerry got out of the truck with a shotgun so I pulled out the SIG she gave me and emptied the clip in him.
Dr. Winter:	You saw him fall?
Player:	Sure. He was lying on the road.

Player reaches across, moves white, Pawn takes Pawn, and hits the chess clock. MC moves the piece on the tournament board.

Celeste:	That was Eric.
Dr. Winter:	Who's Eric?
Celeste:	One of Jerry's guys. Jerry has guys like Eric for stuff like that. They get killed sometimes. It's that kind of business.

That's why I gave him *(points at Player)* the SIG.

Dr. Winter: What's a SIG?

Celeste: A pistol. The one I gave him fires a 9 mil round. That's my favorite. Light, easy to handle.

                Eric stopped showing up about that time. Jerry said he split but he must have been lying.

Raymond moves the black Pawn to Bishop 3 and hits the chess clock. MC moves the piece on the tournament board.

Player: Jerry caught me the week before, when I was leaving her house, and said he was going to kill me.

Celeste: He has a bit of a jealous side.

Player: Caught me at the stoplight, heading out to meet her. Pulled up behind me with those lights going over the roof of my car.

Celeste: That was Jerry's truck. He loves that truck. He had a special lift kit put on it in Houston. A false bottom in the bed. He can carry seventeen kees in the bed of that truck.

Player: You know it seems like everything she says ends up having something to do with moving drugs.

Celeste: *(sarcastic smiling)* Drugs, sex, and guns.

French Defense — The Opening

Dr. Winter: He has a lot of free floating anxiety
                          doesn't he.

Celeste: Yeah. A wacko.

*Player walks over to the chess game, impulsively moves the
white King to Bishop 1, and hits the chess clock. MC moves
the piece on the tournament board.*

Player: Damn. What the hell was that! Now I
                          can't castle. Pawn takes Pawn. Pawn
                          takes Pawn. *(shouting)* Pawn takes Pawn.

Celeste: Are you ok?

Player: Hell no.

*Raymond moves the black Pawn to Bishop3 and hits the
chess clock. MC moves the piece on the tournament board.*

Celeste: Everything is so complicated for you. You
                          even make simple things complicated.

Player: Like what?

Celeste: Buying groceries. You read the labels on
                          everything.

Player: That's just good shopping.

*Player moves the white Knight to Bishop4 and hits the chess
clock. MC moves the piece on the tournament board.*

Celeste: That's not good shopping. Good
                          shopping is fun.

Player: And that's what's wrong with you.
                          Everything has to be fun.

Raymond moves black, Pawn takes Pawn, and hits the chess clock. MC moves the piece on the tournament board.

Celeste: What's the point of breathing if it ain't fun?

Player: Breathing isn't fun. It's just something you have to do.

Player moves white, Knight takes Pawn on 6, and hits the chess clock. MC moves the piece on the tournament board.

Celeste pulls her feet up under her and leans away from Dr. Winter.

Player: You and me are so different. Why do you keep bugging me?

Celeste: Why are you asking me?

Player: You keep bugging me.

Celeste: You left me sitting in my living room and never called. duh. Maybe it pissed me off.

Player: I can't undo that.

Raymond moves the black Knight to Bishop3 and hits the chess clock. MC moves the piece on the tournament board.

Celeste: Me either.

Player: You're driving me nuts with this crap.

Celeste: You were nuts before I met you.

Player moves white, Knight takes Pawn, and hits the chess clock. MC moves the piece on the tournament board.

French Defense – The Opening

Player: Check.

Celeste: I'm really not a bad person, you know.

Raymond moves the black King to Bishop1 and hits the chess clock. MC moves the piece on the tournament board.

Player: I know you're not. But I worry about you.

Celeste: Still my conscience.

Player moves the white Bishop to Rook 6 and hits the chess clock. MC moves the piece on the tournament board.

                   So what's your daughter doing?

Raymond moves the black King to Knight1 and hits the chess clock. MC moves the piece on the tournament board.

                   Kind of avoiding that one aren't you?

Player: No, I'm not. She's about the same.

Player moves the white Queen to Bishop1 on the board and hits the chess clock. MC moves the piece on the tournament board.

Celeste: Same as what?

Player: Working at the mall.

Celeste: Well, that's good. What's she do?

Player: Sells jewelry or something. She has a
                   kiosk.

Celeste: *(sarcastically)* Sounds like you really stay
                   in touch.

Raymond moves the black Pawn to King5 and hits the chess clock. MC moves the piece on the tournament board.

Player: They're growing up. You know how it is.

Player moves the white Queen to Knight5 and hits the chess clock. MC moves the piece on the tournament board.

Celeste: Not really. You going to see 'em for Christmas?

Player: Not this year.

Raymond moves the black King to Bishop2 and hits the chess clock. MC moves the piece on the tournament board.

       They're kind of burned out on being around me. So I'm staying here and let them enjoy their holidays.

       They're going to my folks. Mom makes fudge and banana nut bread at Christmas.

Celeste: My mom couldn't cook a TV dinner. That's what we usually had.

Player: ummh.

       Why'd you get married?

Celeste: Damned if I know. I guess I was in luv. That's about it. It seemed like what I wanted. Why'd you?

Player: Yeah. Same reason I guess. I'm not sure.

French Defense — The Opening

Celeste: It wasn't love at first sight?

Player: I don't remember much about it now. It
                  was all crazy.

Celeste: That's it.

*Player moves the white Knight to Rook5 and hits the chess
clock. MC moves the piece on the tournament board.*

Player: The first few years were ok.

Celeste: That's when we started moving shit to
                  New York. He knew some guys in
                  Laredo.

Player: The next five it went to hell. Ugly. Really
                  ugly.

Celeste: It was better money'n teaching at the
                  junior college. What do you think of this
                  Raymond?

Player: He's just a kid.

Celeste: Remind you of your son?

Player: No. This kid's a biker.

Celeste: *(offended)* What's that mean?

Player: My son's at UCLA. You won't find
                  anybody there like this.

*Raymond moves black, Knight takes Knight, and hits the
chess clock. MC moves the piece on the tournament board.*

Celeste:	So, what's that mean? How do you know. What do you think a biker's like? You know any?
Player:	I've seen them. The Dragons hanging out at the Purple Cow were a rough bunch. Remember them? That's the gang he's in.
Celeste:	How do you know?
Player:	Duh, see the Blood Dragons logo on his jacket? Same bunch. I don't know how he got over here.
Celeste:	On his motorcycle?
Player:	Or how he ended up in this chess club...
Celeste:	...playing chess.

Player moves white, Queen takes Knight, and hits the chess clock. MC moves the piece on the tournament board..

Player:	Check. You're such a comedian. He plays well enough.
Celeste:	There you go. He plays chess so he joined a chess club.

Raymond moves the black King to King2 and hits the chess clock. MC moves the piece on the tournament board.

Player:	Makes sense I guess.
Celeste:	Sure it does. Why else would he be here?

Player moves the white Bishop to King Knight 5 and hits the chess clock. MC moves the piece on the tournament board.

Player: Check. He's dead now.

Raymond moves the black King to Bishop1 and hits the chess clock. MC moves the piece on the tournament board.

Celeste: God. What losers.

Player moves the white Knight to King5 and hits the chess clock. MC moves the piece on the tournament board.

Player: Everybody's a loser someway. someday.

Raymond: Black resigns.

Player: Good game.

Raymond: It was ok.

Player: White always has the advantage.

Raymond: I thought I had you when you moved
                 that king.

Player: Yeah. So, what are you doing in New
                 Orleans?

Raymond: What's it look like, freak?

Player: That's a Blood Dragons jacket you got on.

Raymond: You can read too.

Player: That's a Houston gang. You belong to
                 that gang?

Raymond: It's not a gang. It's a motorcycle club.

Player: Houston's a long way from here.

Raymond:	Not that far. They got roads between Houston and New Orleans.
Player:	What's the difference between a gang and a club?
Raymond:	You're pissin' me off.
Player:	I just wondered why you'd be over here in New Orleans. Since you belong to a Houston motorcycle club and all.
Raymond:	We have a New Orleans chapter.
Player:	You a mechanic?
Raymond:	Sometimes. Mostly though I do airbrush work. Tanks and fenders.
Player:	You ever been down to Angleton?
Raymond:	Sure. I grew up in Lake Jackson. What do you know about Angleton?
Player:	I had a contract down there a year or so back.
Raymond:	Small world ain't it?
Player:	Right. Small world. They had some Dragons that used to hang out not far from where I was staying.
Raymond:	I wouldn't know about that.

Raymond stands up and MC walks over to the table.

MC:	Good game.

Player:	Thanks.
MC:	I have to give you credit for pulling it out at the end. I thought Raymond had you.
	Ok. Player, your next match is with Sam Anzalone on Saturday. 4 in the afternoon. OK?
Player:	Sure. No sweat.
MC:	Raymond. You're playing Spielmann tomorrow.
Raymond:	What time?
MC:	5. Spielmann, you going to be ready?
Spielmann:	I've been practicing.
MC:	Don't forget to show up. Well, gentlemen, good match. I'll have the rankings posted tonight.
Raymond:	See you guys later.
Spielmann:	Guess I better go too. Time to get some supper.

All leave except Celeste, Dr. Winter, and Player who sits at the chess board moving pieces.

Player:	You know I think there's something funny about that Raymond.
Celeste:	You were always paranoid.

Dr. Winter:	We can't do anything to help him until he's ready.
Player:	Take Dr. Head Case with you when you leave.
Celeste:	Be sweet and good, Player.

Celeste and Dr. Winter leave, the lights dim to black.

– French Defense –

Middle Game

Scene I
Repechage

Spielmann, Raymond, and MC are in the chess club. MC is sitting in the armchair reading a chess magazine while he drinks coffee and eats beignets. Spielmann and Raymond are sitting at the center table.

Raymond: Knight to King 8. Checkmate.

Spielmann: That was quick. I didn't even see it coming.

Raymond begins putting the chess pieces away.

You're good.

Raymond: I play a lot. You can't learn it reading chess problems out of the paper.

Spielmann: I need to get one of those chess computers like Player.

Raymond: Humans are better. Machines don't give you the same feel for competition.

Spielmann: Player uses one.

Raymond: He's also nuts. You need experience playing against a human, sweating and stinking across from you. Not a piece of plastic, blinking lights at you.

French Defense — Middle Game

Spielmann: He played pretty well the other day.

Raymond: That was luck.

Spielmann: Why'd you use the French Defense?

Raymond: I thought it would be fun to beat him with it.

Spielmann: But it was his opening.

Raymond: Next time we play I get white. Then we play my opening.

Spielmann: I see.

Raymond: Except with that guy you don't know what he's going to do.

He changed his style in the middle of that game.

Spielmann: He's a wacky guy.

Raymond: Why'd you use the Two Knights?

Spielmann: I like it.

Raymond: But you blocked yourself. Alekhine would be better. You should study that defense.

Spielmann: I'll take a look at it.

Spielmann stands up, goes over to his table, sits down and starts reading his newspaper. MC comes over and sits at the table with Raymond.

MC:	Raymond, have you thought about that tournament in Atlanta?
Raymond:	Looks like I can make it.
MC:	Good. I'll get the registration.

MC leaves the stage and Player walks in with Celeste and Dr. Winter following him. Celeste sits in the arm chair, bottle of Bushmills in one hand and glass in the other. Dr. Winter stands near her. Player walks over to another table and sits down.

Player:	Hey, Raymond.
Raymond:	Player.
Spielmann:	Hello, Player.
Player:	When are we supposed to play again?
Raymond:	Next Wednesday.
Player:	Ok. That's good. You and Spielmann finished?
Spielmann:	Just now.
Player:	Who won?
Spielmann:	Raymond. My Two Knights defense wasn't very good.
Player:	10 moves?
Spielmann:	12.
Player:	That's not bad.

Spielmann: I thought I'd do better.

Raymond: Maybe next time.

MC comes out with the registration form.

MC: Hello, Player. Good match yesterday.

Player: Thanks.

Raymond: You surprised me. I wasn't expecting you to play it that way.

Player: I was trying something different.

MC: *(hands the form to Raymond)* If you could get it back to me tomorrow...

Player: What's that?

MC: An entry form for a tournament.

Player: Which one?

MC: Atlanta. Next month.

Player: Got another one of those? I think I'd like to enter.

MC: That was my last one.

Player: Oh.

MC: I'll give 'em a call and see if they can send me another one.

Player: When's the deadline?

MC:	Next week.
Player:	I see.
MC:	I didn't think you'd be interested. It's a three day tournament.
Player:	So you figured the biker kid would be?

Raymond starts to stand up but MC motions to him to remain seated.

MC:	He's on the way up.
Player:	I beat him yesterday.
MC:	Good game too. But you aren't consistent enough for a tournament.
Player:	That's a bunch of crap.
MC:	Check the rankings. You're fifth in the club.
Player:	I guess biker boy is higher?
MC:	Second.
Player:	Who's first?
MC:	Janice Singleton. But she can't make the trip.
Player:	Janice?
MC:	She's two points ahead of Raymond right now.
Player:	That's 'cause I beat him yesterday.

French Defense — Middle Game

MC: Can you beat him playing black?

Player: Damn straight.

MC: Be interesting to see.

              I'll see what I can do about getting you a
              form. But think about it. It won't be like
              playing in the club here.

MC goes back to his office to order another entry form.
Player leans over to look at the form in Raymond's hand.

Player: I could have just copied this one. I bet
              they'd have taken it.

Raymond: He's already got most of it filled in.

Player: I bet we could have copied it.

Raymond: You're a freak you know that?

Player: I'm no freak.

Player goes over to another table and sits with his chess
computer. Raymond fills in the rest of the form.

Spielmann: What kind of chess computer is that?

Player: It's a 2000Tal.

Spielmann: Is that a good one?

Player: I wouldn't own it if it wasn't.

Spielmann: I've been thinking about getting one.

Player: You should. It helps get ready for these
              tournaments.

Spielmann: Raymond said it wasn't as good as
              playing a person.

Player: Sounds like him. He's kind of strange like
              that. But it's always hard finding
              somebody to practice with. Beats the hell
              out of those chess problems in the paper.

Spielmann: Maybe I will. If I don't move to Florida.

MC walks out.

MC: OK Player. I called the club and they
              faxed me another form.

MC hands Player a registration form.

              Get that back to me tomorrow and I'll
              send it in for you.

Player: Great. Thanks, MC

Raymond: Here you go, MC

Raymond hands him the form and a handful of bills.

MC: Thanks. *(counts the money)* I'll get this
              out in the morning.

Raymond: See you guys later. I'm going to hit the
              street.

MC: Sure thing. Good match today.

*Player and Spielmann lift their hands in a small salute.
Player fills out his form and holds it out toward MC.*

Player: Here's mine.

French Defense — Middle Game

MC: You got fifty?

Player: Sure. But I got to go down to the ATM.

MC: Ok, I'll wait.

Player gets up and hurries out of the room. Celeste and Dr. Winter follow him out.

Spielmann: You know he talks to his chess computer?

MC: I've heard him mumbling sometimes. How do you know he's talking to his computer?

Spielmann: He called it Celeste yesterday.

MC: He's a strange one. I don't think he's up to playing in a rated tournament. But nothing was going to stop him.

Spielmann: He was good yesterday.

MC: One day. One match.
Hey, you never know, maybe he'll do ok.

Spielmann: Do you ever play in these tournaments?

MC: Not me. It's not good for my heart.

Spielmann: You're young to be having heart trouble.

MC: Yeah.

Spielmann: What kind of trouble?

MC: I had a bypass last year.

Spielmann:	How old are you?
MC:	A little over 50.
Spielmann:	You're too young.
MC:	It's a family thing. Dad didn't make it past 48.
Spielmann:	Geez. What'd he do, smoke?
MC:	No. Or drink. It's just genetic.
Spielmann:	What about exercise?
MC:	Everyday. He was a bodybuilder.
Spielmann:	That's not aerobic.
MC:	You ever lift weights?
Spielmann:	No. Not me.
MC:	I do. You can get your pulse rate up if you don't rest too long between sets.
Spielmann:	But they say...
MC:	Yeah. That's what *they* say. Whoever *they* are. You ever know who *they* are?
Spielmann:	Doctors.
MC:	Name one.
Spielmann:	I heard it on the news. One of those news shows.

MC: You heard 'em say coffee was bad for you too?

Spielmann: That's what they say.

MC: You ever see anybody drop dead drinking a cup of coffee?

Spielmann: No.

MC: Be a lot of dead folks in those coffee shops if that was true.

Spielmann: But it's the long term effects...

MC: How long?

Spielmann: ...they're talking about...

MC: A day?

Spielmann: ... a long time.

MC: Six years?

Spielmann: A long time.

MC: Then it could be anything. Maybe it's actually aspirin. I bet all of those heart attack victims took aspirin too.

Spielmann: That's supposed to be good for you.

MC: Who says?

Spielmann: Ok, ok. But I don't believe it's genetics. There's got to be a reason.

MC: You don't think that's a reason?

Spielmann: No.

MC: Why?

Spielmann: Because something caused it. Fatty food.
               Not enough exercise. Something.

MC: Ever heard "shit happens?"

Spielmann: I see it on bumper stickers.

MC: You don't believe in chance? Living in
               New Orleans?

Spielmann: I believe in controlling life.

MC: Right up to the point when the asteroid
               smacks your brains out.

Spielmann: Damn that's morbid.

MC: I guess it is. I'm just in a bit of a mood is
               all.

Spielmann: You got kids?

MC: A son.

Spielmann: How old?

MC: He's going to college up at Hammond.

Spielmann: So where is Hammond?

MC: North of the lake.

Spielmann: I've never been up there.

MC: They got a state college up there. He's majoring in agriculture.

Spielmann: I don't know anything about farming. I grew up in New York. City.

MC: My mother was from New York.

Spielmann: Really.

MC: A little town up the Hudson.

Spielmann: They've got some nice little villages up there. How'd she end up down here?

MC: My dad got transferred down here when I was a kid. So we moved. He worked for Chrysler.

Spielmann: Where's he from?

MC: Canada. Windsor, Ontario.

Spielmann: I didn't know Chrysler made cars in New Orleans.

MC: They didn't. It was Saturn boosters. For the Apollo program.

Spielmann: I didn't know they did that either.

MC: He was an engineer. They made the external tank for the shuttle. But it's not the same as back when they were making boosters for the Apollo program.

Spielmann: I didn't know anything about it.

MC:	That's how it is here. The only thing you hear about around here is the French Quarter, restaurants, and Marie Laveau.
Spielmann:	That's the voodoo lady, right?
MC:	How long you lived in New Orleans?
Spielmann:	Not long.
MC:	You said you were a retired teacher.
Spielmann:	Sure. When I retired I moved here from Houston.
MC:	Seems like we got our share of people from Houston over here lately.
Spielmann:	We used to come over here for vacation alot. My daughter lives in Florida so it's closer to her.
MC:	Why not just go ahead and move on to Florida like all the other retirees?
Spielmann:	I didn't want to live *that* close to her. She drives me nuts. This way I'm only a few hours away. That's close enough for me.
MC:	You ever go down to the Quarter?
Spielmann:	Not much lately. Since my wife died I don't get out much.
MC:	Where do you live?
Spielmann:	I'm out in Kenner.
MC:	Man, that's a drive getting over here.

Spielmann: I don't mind. This is all I have to do anymore. What about you?

MC: I live in Metairie.

Spielmann: Nice area.

MC: I like it. How'd you end up teaching school in Houston?

Player comes walking into the room at a brisk pace and out of breath. Celeste and Dr. Winter enter and take up their previous places.

Player: Ok, I got it. *(hands the money to MC)* Am I set?

MC counts the money.

MC: You're set. I'll get this off to Atlanta first thing in the morning.

Player: Thanks. This is going to be great.

MC: It's almost time to lock up for the evening. 30 more minutes.

Spielmann: I guess I'm done. See you guys tomorrow.

Spielmann gathers his things and leaves.

Player: Let me know when you want to lock up.

Celeste walks over and sits at the table with Player. Player doesn't look up at her. She watches him. Dr. Winter walks up and stands behind her watching Player move the pieces on his chess board. The lights dim to black.

Scene II
Steinitz Variation

The lights come up and Celeste is sitting in the armchair, Bushmills bottle by the chair, glass in her hand. Dr. Winter is standing near her. Player sits at the center chess table facing the audience. The lighting and makeup cast dark shadows across his face.

Raymond is sitting at the center chess table with his back to the audience. In the back is the large wall mounted tournament chessboard. MC stands by the board and moves the "pieces." Celeste now announces all of Raymond's moves after he makes them.

Raymond moves white Pawn to King 4 and hits the chess clock. MC moves the piece on the tournament chessboard.

Celeste:	White moves Pawn to King 4. You haven't played chess lately.
Player:	This is the first time since the tournament.
Celeste:	Why not?
Player:	I make mistakes now.
Celeste:	You used to be pretty good.
Player:	How's your daughter?
Celeste:	She's fine. She's started Junior High.
Player:	Junior High.

Celeste: Yeah. Junior High. She has a couple of little boy friends.

Player: She's growing up.

Celeste: Yeah.

Player: Did you ever go on your trip?

Celeste: Not yet.

Player: Still running? Pawn to King 3.

Player moves black Pawn to King 3 and hits the chess clock. MC moves the piece on the tournament board.

Celeste: And teaching. Life is good.

Player: No Feds?

Celeste: Not yet.

Raymond moves the white Pawn to Queen 4 and hits the chess clock. MC moves the piece on the tournament board.

        White, Pawn to Queen 4. But it's getting tougher. I got to admit. We're only moving half what we did last year.

Celeste sips from her glass.

Player: Why don't 'cha quit.

Celeste: I've been thinking about it. But too many people want me to stay in. They get nervous when I bring it up.

Player: What's next?

Celeste: I'm not sure. It's not the kind of thing
                you just walk away from.

Player: What about your daughter? Pawn to
                Queen 4.

*Player moves the black Pawn to Queen 4 and hits the chess
clock. MC moves the piece on the tournament board.*

Celeste: So. What about you? What're you doing?

Player: Nothing much lately. I haven't been able
                to line up any contracts since the Norco
                job.

Celeste: How long ago was that?

Player: *(looks down at his trembling hands)* A few
                months now.

Celeste: How're you getting by?

Player: *(shrugs without looking up)* I cut back.

*Raymond moves the white Knight to QueenBishop 3 and hits
the chess clock. MC moves the piece on the tournament
board.*

Celeste: White, Knight to QueenBishop 3. Where
                are you staying?

Player: I got a room. Not far from here.

Celeste: You don't look so good.

Player: I'm fine.

                I was thinking about Surfside today. I
                really miss living on the beach. I think

that was probably the best time I ever had.

Knight to KingBishop 3.

Player moves the black Knight to KingBishop 3 and hits the chess clock. MC moves the piece on the tournament board.

Raymond moves the white Pawn to King 5 and hits the chess clock. MC moves the piece on the tournament board.

Celeste: White, Pawn to King 5. It wasn't that great.

Player: Sure it was.

Celeste: You should come on back then.

Player: I can't.

Celeste: Nobody cares what you did. Hell, nobody even remembers.

Player: Once you leave you can't go back.

My momma used to say that a lot. KingKnight to Queen 2.

Player moves the black KingKnight to Queen 2 and hits the chess clock. MC moves the piece on tournament board.

Celeste: That's why you're nuts. You got to let that stuff go.

Player: I'm getting tired of people saying I'm nuts.

Celeste: You're just a bit obsessive. How's that?

Player:	Better, I think.

Celeste:	Well, you are obsessive. Little things bug you that I don't even notice.

Player:	That's why I'm a good chemist.

Raymond moves the QueenKnight to King and hits the chess clock. MC moves the piece on the tournament board.

Celeste:	White, QueenKnight to King 2. God that's depressing. Why don't you call me? You should come back.

Player:	I can't. Pawn to QueenBishop 4.

Player moves the black Pawn to QueenBishop 4 and hits the chess clock. MC moves the piece on the tournament board.

Celeste:	Why not?

Celeste sips her whiskey and looks at Dr. Winter.

	You talk to him. He's just shining me on.

Dr. Winter:	What's wrong with him?

Player:	I'm a little burned out. That's all. Just a little burned out.

Dr. Winter:	It happens. I didn't play much after Ruth died.

Player:	I've been tired since the Atlanta tournament.

Dr. Winter:	What have you been doing?

Player:	Mostly I just sit here and study the board.
Dr. Winter:	That's intersesting. Why do you still come here?
Player:	I like being around the boards. Especially during the week when they're empty.
Dr. Winter:	But all you've been doing is sitting there.
Player:	Maybe it's the quiet.

Raymond moves the white Pawn to QueenBishop 3 and hits the chess clock. MC moves the piece on the tournament board.

Celeste:	White, Pawn to QueenBishop 3.
Player:	I've been thinking.
Dr. Winter:	About what?
Player:	Lots of things. Knight to QueenBishop 3.

Player moves the black Knight to QueenBishop 3 and hits the chess clock. MC moves the piece on the tournament board.

Dr. Winter:	Not much of an answer.
Player:	Things. How's that?
Dr. Winter:	Cute. Name something.
Player:	The Gulf of Mexico. Early in the morning. Sun on the water.
Dr. Winter:	That's a start.

Raymond moves the white Pawn to KingBishop 4 and hits the chess clock. MC moves the piece on the tournament board.

Celeste: White, Pawn to KingBishop 4.

Player: Once, when I was living in Surfside, one morning before I left for work I saw a whale stranded in the shallows.

                  I'd never seen that in person before. Live. The wind was coming in off the Gulf. It was a beautiful morning. Pawn to Bishop 3.

Player moves the black Pawn to Bishop 3 and hits the chess clock. MC moves the piece on the tournament board.

Dr. Winter: What happened?

Raymond moves the white Knight to Bishop 3 and hits the chess clock. MC moves the piece on the tournament board.

Celeste: White, Knight to Bishop 3.

Player: It died. An aquarium in Galveston came down the island late in the day to get it. But it was dead by the time they got there.

                  I think it was sick. That's why it was in the shallows. Queen to Knight 3.

Player moves the black Queen to Knight 3 and hits the chess clock. MC moves the piece on the tournament board.

Celeste: I remember that.

Dr. Winter: Sad.

Player:	Yeah. When I lived in L.A. you'd hear about that happening sometimes. It was always sad.
	Hey, you guys. You're screwing up my game.
Celeste:	We're just watching.
Player:	And talking. I'm trying to beat this kid so shut up. Just be over there and shut up.
Spielmann:	I lived in L.A. Back in the 50's.
Player:	*(turns and looks at Spielmann)* What?
Spielmann:	You said you lived in L.A. I did too.
Raymond:	Ok, freaks. Knock it off. We're playing chess here, not socializing.
Player:	Talking bothers you?
Raymond:	This here's a chess club.

Raymond moves the white Pawn to QueenRook3 and hits the chess clock. MC moves the piece on the tournament board.

Celeste:	White, Pawn to QueenRook3.
Player:	Then I guess it's not what you expected.
Raymond:	Are you playing or talking?
Player:	Playing. Bishop to King 2.

Player moves the black Bishop to King 2 and hits the chess clock. MC moves the piece on the tournament board.

Dr. Winter: I lived in California too.

Player: How'd you end up out there?

Dr. Winter: When I got back from Korea in '53, I decided I liked the weather. So I stayed.

Player: You were in Korea?

Dr. Winter: Marines, 1st Division. Made the landing at Inchon.

Celeste: So was my dad. Used to say Korea was the coldest he'd ever been. Colder'n a witches tit.

That's what he'd say.

Dr. Winter: It was. Damn near froze my ass off. Almost lost my toes.

Raymond moves the white Pawn to QueenKnight 4 and hits the chess clock. MC moves the piece on the tournament board.

Celeste: White, Pawn to QueenKnight 4.

Player: I was 1st Division. Iraq. It was hot as hell but dry. Started sweating when we got off the transport and didn't stop till I left.

Couldn't see it though. It just evaporated. Had sweat grub on my skin the whole time. Pawn takes QueenPawn.

Player moves black, Pawn takes QueenPawn, and hits the chess clock. MC moves the corresponding piece on the wall mounted tournament chessboard.

French Defense – Middle Game

Celeste:	Dad was at Chosin. He told me there were a million Chinese.
Dr. Winter:	They hit in waves at night. Bunch of teenagers, we'd never seen anything like it.
Celeste:	He thought they were all going to die.
Dr. Winter:	After I got back I drank hard for a long time. Until somebody called me an alcoholic.
Celeste:	But you're a shrink.
Dr. Winter:	A drunk shrink for years. But I quit it in 67.
	Still an alcoholic though.

Raymond moves white, Pawn takes QueenPawn, and hits the chess clock. MC moves the piece on the tournament board.

Celeste:	White, Pawn takes QueenPawn.
Dr. Winter:	You drinking?
Player:	A little.
Raymond:	Hey. You keep talking and I'm going to punch your face in.
Player:	I was just thinking out loud. Black castles.

Player moves black, Black castles Kingside, and hits the chess clock. MC moves the corresponding piece on the wall mounted tournament chessboard.

Raymond:	Shut up.
MC:	You fellas ok over there?
Raymond:	He keeps talking to himself.
Player:	I was just thinking out loud. That's all.
Raymond:	You're a freak.
Player:	I'm no freak.
Spielmann:	I don't think Player's feeling well.
Player:	There's nothing wrong with me.
Spielmann:	You're talking to your chess computer.
Player:	So what. Nothing wrong with that.
Spielmann:	People don't talk to machines.
Player:	Bullshit.
Spielmann:	You named it. That's not normal.
Player:	What are you talking about?
Spielmann:	Celeste.
Player:	I don't call my computer Celeste.
Spielmann:	I've heard you.
Player:	You're crazy.
MC:	*(reprimanding)* Gentlemen. This is a chess club not a kindergarten.

French Defense – Middle Game

Raymond: Tell freak to shut up while we're playing.

MC: Player.

Player: I didn't realize I was talking out loud.

Raymond: If he does it again I'm going to shove this board down his goddamn throat.

MC: Maybe you two should take a break and finish this game tomorrow.

Player: I'm ok.

MC: I'd rather you take the break.

Raymond: Sure thing, chief.

MC walks up to their table.

MC: I'll leave everything the way it is and you can pick it up again tomorrow.

Raymond: I can do that.

Player: Yeah.

MC: Player you don't look so good. Are you alright?

Player: I'm fine, doc.

Player stands up and starts walking for the door.

MC: You leaving for the day?

Player: You got it. I think I'll go get something to eat. Be back tomorrow.

Raymond:	Don't get lost, freak.
Player:	I won't, punk.

Player leaves the club followed by Celeste and Dr. Winter.

Raymond:	That's one bizarre human being.
MC:	You should let that stuff slide. You can't play chess if you're twisted around the axle.
Raymond:	That guy just pisses me off.
MC:	I've noticed. He's noticed too.
Spielmann:	Did you see his face? I bet he's a solo drinker.
MC:	Could be. But it's not my business.
Spielmann:	I've never seen anybody fall apart like this.
Raymond:	I seen worse. He don't stink bad enough yet. When you start smelling it coming through his skin then you know he's hit bottom.
Spielmann:	Somebody ought to do something.
Raymond:	You sound like a frikin' social worker. What was it you did before you retired?
Spielmann:	I was a teacher.
Raymond:	What'd you teach?
Spielmann:	Math.

French Defense – Middle Game

Raymond: High school?

Spielmann: Junior High.

Raymond: I hated every math teacher I ever had.

Spielmann: Doesn't surprise me. Guess I'll get on
                home. See you fellas tomorrow.

Spielmann leaves.

Raymond: Guess he didn't like the comment about
                not liking math teachers.

MC: It wasn't something I'd have told him.

Raymond: Hey. That's me. Mr. Bad Example.

MC: How'd it go this weekend?

Raymond: I kicked ass. It was just local talent
                though, nothing worldclass.

MC: Make any money?

Raymond: A little. But most everybody up there was
                just playing for fun. Boring.

MC: I got a call yesterday about a guy that
                wants to play a private match.

Raymond: Sounds fun. Who is it?

MC: I can't say. It's a high stakes game
                though.

Raymond: Some rich dude?

MC: He's got money. You interested?

Raymond: What's the stakes?

MC: 50k.

Raymond: That's steep.

MC: It's not speed chess.

Raymond: Hell, that could take days.

MC: I told him I didn't think you'd be
               interested.

Raymond: Right. I think I'll pass on this one.

MC: Ok. I'll check with Janis.

               How's the bike club going?

Raymond: Pretty good. We got a chapter starting up
               in Pensacola next month.

MC: What do these chapters do?

Raymond: Get together and ride their bikes.
               Weekend trips. Stuff like that.

MC: Seems like they wouldn't need a club to
               do that.

Raymond: We get 'em set up with their gear and
               make the connections for them. Making
               sure they got all their permits and stuff.

MC: What's the Houston club get? There's got
               to be money in it somehow. Where's the
               money?

Raymond: There's a percentage on the stuff they buy. But it's the dues.

MC: How much are the dues?

Raymond: I ain't talking no more about the club.

MC: That's ok. I was just curious, that's all.

Raymond: That can get you into trouble sometimes if you're not careful.

MC: Forget I asked. I'm not that interested.

Raymond: Let's just say the club back in Houston does ok.

MC: Good enough.

Does everybody ride those Harley's?

Raymond: Most of us do. But over here there's some Jap bikes in the mix, a few old Nortons, and one guy has a Triumph.

MC: Nortons used to be good bikes.

Raymond: Good on the strip but not so great on these long rides we pull now days.

MC: What about BMWs?

Raymond: Oh man. I think the crew would beat the shit out of anybody showing up on one of those German bikes. The Jap bikes are bad enough but at least they pretend to look like hogs. The ones in our club any-way.

MC:	So you don't like those Ninja bikes?
Raymond:	That's plastic crap, man. All revs and no balls.
MC:	Is that the deal with the BMWs?
Raymond:	They're slick. But, hell, you might as well be in a car. Nobody in the club would respect you running around on something like that. That'd be like wearing a three piece suit on a ride.
MC:	I thought you had some professionals in your club?
Raymond:	But you're missing the point, MC. Nobody wants to be like that when they're on their bike.
MC:	You really like this motorcycle stuff don't you.
Raymond:	They're my brothers, man.
MC:	That's different from here? *(he motions around the room)*
Raymond:	You know what I mean. In here I'm kicking ass. I ain't got any friends in here except you.
MC:	Thanks. But these guys should be your friends.
Raymond:	Not when I'm going to rip their ass. I'm only here to play chess, but the bike club is something else.

MC: I don't play chess here.

I guess I've noticed people in the club really aren't friends with each other.

Raymond: Except that dick, Spielmann. That's what makes him out of place. Like a cop trying to fit into something he doesn't understand.

MC: He's just lonely.

Raymond: Believe what you want.

MC: Thought any more about going to college?

Raymond: I got too much going on right now to do that.

MC: Well, I'm not going to give up on you.

Raymond: Just don't bug me about it.

MC: I won't.

MC holds out his hand and he and Raymond shake hands.

Let's get out of here. I want to go home and get some supper.

Raymond: Sounds like a plan.

Raymond collects his things and MC waits. Lights fade to black as they leave the stage.

End Game

Scene I
The Black Cat Club

A French Quarter Bar with The Best of Warren Zevon playing in the background. There are a handful of bar tables and a small platform for an exotic dancer in the back. In place of the sign saying "Paul Morphy Chess Club" is a sign that says "The Black Cat Club."

There is a dim spotlight on the platform and Celeste, now an exotic dancer named Lisa, is wearing a leopard skin bikini and dancing on the platform - it's the same bump and grind regardless of the song that's playing.

Player sits at the center table, dim spotlight, glass on the table is half full, not watching Celeste dance, so drunk his head is down staring at the table. Raymond sits at a table in a dark corner watching Player. There is a bar in front of bookshelves that hold bottles of whiskey. Dr. Winter, now the Bartender, wipes the bar, pours drinks, and cleans glasses.

MC walks in, stops, and looks around the room. When Raymond sees MC, he backs deeper into the shadows so that he can't be seen. When MC sees Player sitting at a table, he walks over.

MC: Well, it's not the Sazerac. Is it.

Player looks up, squinting at MC, and tries to focus.

                I got your message.

Player: *(suddenly smiling)* Hi there, MC.
                Welcome to the Black Cat. Have a seat.

MC sits in one of the chairs at Player's table.

MC: You know, I don't come down here very often.

Player: You should. It's a real change of pace.

MC: *(looks at Celeste dancing on the stage)* I can see that.

      What was it you wanted?

Player: Now hold on a minute. First I'm buying you a drink. What'cha drinkin.

MC: Nothing. I don't want anything.

Player: Sure you do.

Player stands up, swaying a bit, and starts for the bar.

      You look like a martini drinker to me.

MC: That's ok. I really don't want anything.

Player ignores him and makes it to the bar.

Player: One martini. *(he turns to MC and shouts)* Vodka?

MC: Ok. But just one.

Player: Olive or onion?

MC: Lemon twist.

Player: You're not going to get that in this dump.

MC: Do the best you can. I'll pretend.

Player: *(turns back to the bartender)* You got
               that?

Bartender: Man wants a Left Bank martini. Stoli or
               Smirnof?

MC: Smirnof.

*Dr. Winter mixes a martini, pours it into a martini glass and
hands it to Player. Player puts a few dollars on the bar, picks
up the drink, and goes back to the table.*

*The bartender picks up the money, counts it, gives Player a
scowl, turns around to put it away, then wipes the bar and
watches Celeste dance.*

MC: Ok. Why was it you wanted me to come
               down here?

Player: How's the drink?

MC: *(sips it)* It's good.

Player: I'm surprised.

MC: *(sips his drink)* Why's that?

Player: Beer and straight shots' about all
               anybody asks for in here.

MC: Sounds like you're a regular.

Player: Not that often, just every now and then. I
               live up the street from here.

MC: Really? Where?

Player:	Off Royal.
MC:	I thought you were over by Tulane.
Player:	I had to let it go.
MC:	Sorry to hear it. Times are tough?
Player:	A bit. Everything is slow right now.
MC:	Where are you working?
Player:	I've got a line on a contract in Texas. Looks I'm going back down there again.
MC:	You'll have to get sober.
Player:	I'm ok. I'm a little buzzed right now but I'll be fine tomorrow. Just celebrating a little tonight.
MC:	What was it you needed to ask me?
Player:	I need a few bucks to get over to Freeport for this contract. I'm just a little short right now. Just a little. Enough for a bus ticket. That's all I need.
MC:	You can't buy a bus ticket? What are you doing in here?
Player:	I was just waiting for you. I didn't want to come by the chess club.
	I didn't want any of the guys seeing me right now. Not being down.
MC:	*(sighs)* How much is a ticket?

Player:	85. It's only 85. And I can pay you back right away. The contract pays weekly. And I got a good rate.
MC:	How long's it going to last?
Player:	They said 3 months. But last time I was there it went a year. That's how these things are. You never know.
	But it's at least a 3 month. I was there once before and it went for a year.
MC:	When are you leaving?
Player:	I'm just waiting on the call. They said they'd know by tomorrow. But they've had this one on hold so long it's going to happen.
MC:	Ok, then.
	You know, I try not to get involved. But you look like hell.
	Tell you what I'll do. When they give you the word, let me know and I'll come by, take you down to the bus station and buy you the ticket.
Player:	I was hoping I could borrow the money from you tonight. So I could get my ticket now and then I'd be ready first thing tomorrow.
	That's how these things are.
MC:	But you don't have a contract yet.

Player: I will tomorrow when they call. And then I could just get on the bus and I'd be there ready for Monday.

MC: I'm not going to give you any money.

Player: But you...

MC: ...said I'll buy you the ticket and put you on the bus. But I'm not giving you any money. I wasn't born last night you know. *(motions around the room)* You'd drink it and *(looking at Celeste)* that'd be the end of it...

Player: Bastard. All I need's bus money to Freeport.

MC: If you don't dry out you aren't going to make it to Freeport.

Player: Don't worry about me. I already worked with these guys. They know I'm good.

MC: Were good. Right now you're barely able to stagger over to that bar.

Player: *(offended)* I expected more support from you. I'm a member.

MC: You haven't paid your dues lately.

Player: I've been having rough times. *(tries to brighten up)* But after I get this contract I'll get everything squared away.

MC: I hope so. *(finishes his martini)* Good martini.

Look, I've got to get back to the club. Call me tomorrow about the contract. If it comes thorough I'll be happy to buy you the ticket.

And it won't be a loan.

Player: I don't want any money from you.

MC: You give me a call.

Player: Yeah, right.

MC stands up and puts a few bills on the table.

MC: Thanks for the drink. I haven't had one in a long time. *(looking at Celeste)* Interesting place too.

See you around.

Player: Wait a minute. Don't go yet. I wanted to ask you about the guys. Com'on, sit down a minute.

How's old Spielmann doing?

MC: I really have to get back. There's another round robin...

Player: Is Janice still number one?

MC: Yes. She's got a ten point lead on Raymond. He's number two now.

Player: What about Spielmann?

MC: He's getting better. He was able to draw a couple of games this time.

Player:	That's good. He's still talking about his daughter?
MC:	Every day. Raymond thinks he's a cop.
Player:	Me too.
MC:	You guys. You sound paranoid. Spielmann's no cop.
Player:	Maybe.
MC:	He's just a lonely old fart.
Player:	Never know. Want another drink?
MC:	No. I got to get back. Call me tomorrow.

MC leaves and Player sits drinking.

At the end of the song, Celeste (now an exotic dancer named Lisa) stops dancing and walks over to Player's table. She holds out a jar containing bills and change.

Celeste:	Got something for the jukebox?
Player:	No. Nothing tonight.
Celeste:	Com'on. You don't want me to stop dancing do you?
Player:	That's ok. Once I finish this drink, I'm going to be leaving.
Celeste:	Cheap shit.

She makes the rounds to the other tables before she stops and sits at a table back in a dark corner. There's a shadow of a figure sitting there. She raises her arm and waves toward the Bartender.

The Bartender reaches under the bar, takes out a bottle of cola, pours it into a glass, and takes it to Celeste.

He stops at Player's table on the way back to the bar.

Bartender: You can't sit in here if you're not buying.

Player: Maybe another beer.

Bartender returns to the bar, pulls out a bottle of beer, and puts it on the bar. Player staggers over, puts two bills down, and takes a sip.

Player: Thanks.

Bartender: You're shorting me on tips.

Player: I'll make it up next week. I got a big
                    contract coming up.

Bartender: Sure, but I'd rather get my money up
                    front.

Player: It's the best I can do tonight.

Bartender: What kind of contract?

Player: Chemist at a refinery in Texas.

Bartender: Oh. That kind of contract.

Player: Yeah.

Bartender: Then it don't pay as good.

Player: But it pays longer.

Bartender:	I don't know. We got some around here that been getting paid good for a long time now. Like the guy over there *(he points to the shadow in the dark corner where Celeste is sitting)* with Lisa.
Player:	That's Celeste.
Bartender:	Whatever. I know her as Lisa. Anyway he's had some good contracts off and on now for almost ten years.
Player:	That's not so long.
Bartender:	It is for some lines of work.
Player:	That's my point.
Bartender:	I don't know anybody that ain't dying. The only question is how good you got it before it happens. Getting whacked fast might not be such a bad thing, you know? My mother-in-law, she had this pancreas cancer. Oh my god that was living hell. I'd rather take a bullet to the brain than go out that way.
Player:	How do you know that doesn't hurt as bad?
Bartender:	Maybe it does. But damn, at least it don't last as long.
Player:	I guess not.
Bartender:	That poor woman. I tell you, towards the end we were giving her massive pain

meds just to try to help put her out it was
so bad.

You know what I mean?

Player: Yeah.

Bartender: She just hung around. I wouldn't wish
that on my worse enemy.

Player: My dad died in his sleep. That was a
good way.

Bartender: It's not a bad one.

Player: No. Not too bad. His old heart just
stopped beating.

Bartender: You ever wonder if you were having a
dream and it happened, would you know
the difference?

Player: Only if there's something after this.

Bartender: You talking about there not being no life
after dying?

Player: Yeah. If it's nothing afterwards then the
dream just ends and you're gone.

Bartender: Jeez. I don't even want to think about it.

Player: Would you rather take your chances on
hell or nothing?

Bartender: I ain't going to hell. I never done
anything bad.

Really bad.

	Just the usual stuff. You think this might be all there is to it?
Player:	Could be. You know, the Jews didn't believe in any of that stuff about going to a heaven after you died.
Bartender:	*(sarcastically)* What do you know about it? You're not a Jew. Besides it's in the Bible.
Player:	Just the Christian part of it. That's the New Testament part. I was in the seminary once for a few years.
Bartender:	Well, I don't read it enough to know.
Player:	It was the Egyptians believed in heaven.
Bartender:	What about hell? Where'd that come from?
Player:	That was the Greeks. Hades. We got hell from them.
Bartender:	You're bullshitting me.
Player:	Tell you what. When you get home you get out your Bible, if you have one, and see if you can find anything in the Old Testament about going to heaven or hell when you die.
Bartender:	Damn. You got me curious now. If I had one in here I'd be looking it up right now.
Player:	How'd we get off on this anyway?

Bartender:	We were talking about killing somebody on a contract.
Player:	Yeah, that was it. Well, I'm not that kind of contractor. I'm just a chemist. So I live longer and make more money.
	Eventually.
Bartender:	Not if you get hit by a car when you stagger out of this joint tonight.
Player:	Point. Good point.
Bartender:	I think it's best just to go for it and get what you can before you kick.
Player:	What about hell?
Bartender:	Maybe there ain't no hell. And there you'd be. Spending your life being good for nothing.
Player:	You sound like a confused hedonist.
Bartender:	I don't know about that stuff. I just mix drinks for a living. *(looks hard at Player)* And try to collect my tips.
Player:	Tell you what. After I get this contract I'll settle up on your tips with interest. How's that?
Bartender:	Pretty much what they all say. Nobody ever settles up on tips.
	(he wipes down the top of the bar with his towel)

What do you think. You think there's something after this? Or do we just snuff out.

Player: I don't know.

Bartender: I'd hate to think that this was it.

Player: It might be a relief to just fade out. Ever think about it like that?

Bartender: Hell, I never think about shit like that.

You know, you're kind of a freak.

Player: That's what I keep hearing.

Celeste gets back up on the stage and begins dancing. Player turns to watch her.

This is a crazy life, isn't it.

Bartender: You talking about that reincarnation crap?

Player: No, no. I was just thinking out loud. You just don't know how things are going to go in life. That's all.

Nothing about reincarnation. Where'd that come from? Although it fits with all the talk about heaven and hell.

Bartender: No. I've had enough about that. Just drink your beer and keep what you're thinking in your own head.

Player: You ever play chess?

Bartender:	Some. When I was in grammar school or maybe junior high.
Player:	I belong to that chess club over on Lee Circle.
Bartender:	Didn't know they had one.
Player:	The Paul Morphy Chess Club.
Bartender:	You mean Murphy.
Player:	No. It's Morphy.
Bartender:	Never heard of it.
Player:	Morphy was from New Orleans. Long time back.
Bartender:	Probably before my time.
Player:	You could say that.
Bartender:	So what's your point about this chess club. Sounds kind of candy-ass to me.
Player:	Outside the club you might think that. Inside it's a different story. Chess is serious business if you're on the inside.
Bartender:	It's a war game right?
Player:	Maybe a thousand or 3 or 4 hundred years ago. But right now I think guns, nukes, and jets sort of screwed that part of it up. And life's unpredictable, if you were going to say it's a metaphor for life. That's about as far away as you can get from good chess.

Bartender:	What the hell are you talking about anyway?
Player:	I'm thinking chess is just a game.
Bartender:	Well, that's what it is.
Player:	A game. It doesn't really mean anything.
Bartender:	Seems kind of obvious to me.
Player:	You'd be surprised how hard it is to see it that way inside the club.
Bartender:	You're nuts. You ought to go do something else for awhile. Forget that chess stuff. You're too old to be playing games.
Player:	Thanks. I'm going to figure you meant mature when you called me old.
Bartender:	Yeah. That's it. So, this contract, what part of Texas is it?
Player:	It's down in south Texas, on the coast.
Bartender:	Sounds nice. Any mosquitoes?
Player:	Enough to pack you away. I thought we had 'em bad here. But that was the worst I've ever seen.
	I was staying in a little town called Klute at first.
Bartender:	That's a Paul Newman movie ain't it?

Player: This was a town. Besides I think it was
               Donald Sutherland and Bridget Fonda in
               that movie.

Bartender: Lisa would know. She knows all about
               movies. We'll get her over here. *(he
               waves Lisa/Celeste over to the bar)* She'll
               know.

Player: I already said. It was Donald Sutherland
               and Bridget Fonda.

Lisa/Celeste walks over to the bar.

Bartender: You said "I think it was." I don't know
               about you, but that's not very sure in my
               book.

Celeste: What is it, baby?

Bartender: You know who was in that *Klute* movie?

Celeste: Jane Fonda, Donald Sutherland, Roy
               Scheider, Rita Gam, Charles Cioffi,
               Nathan George, Dorothy Tristan, and
               Jean Stapleton.

Player: Damn. Jean Stapleton?

Bartender: I told you Lisa would know. She knows
               all about movies.

Celeste: Those were the main actors. Andy and
               David Lewis wrote it. The only film I can
               recall that they got credits for.

Player: Ok, that's enough. I give.

Celeste: So what's this about. Got a bet going or something?

Bartender: No, nothing like that. I thought Paul Newman was in it. You know, one of those loner flicks he used to make.

Celeste: Like *Hud*?

Bartender: That's right. Wasn't there one he made called *Klute*? Or something like that.

Celeste: I don't think so, baby.

Bartender: Damn.

Player: Your name's Celeste?

Celeste: It's Lisa.

Player: Sorry. You look like somebody I used to know.

Celeste: That's an old one.

Player: So how is it you know all those details about movies?

Celeste: I like old movies.

She goes back up on the stage and starts her dance again.

Bartender: Guess you struck out on that line.

Player: That's ok. I'm just a drunk in a bar.

Player finishes off his beer.

	I'll have that extra tip money for you next week.
Bartender:	About the time hell freezes over.
Player:	You can tell her I'll have some money for her jukebox, too. See you around.

Player salutes him and leaves the bar. Raymond walks up to the bar.

Raymond:	That guy come in here very often?
Bartender:	Maybe.
Raymond:	Don't screw around with me, pop.

Raymond puts his hands up on the bar, ready to grab the bartender.

	I'm going to be nice again. That guy come in here very often?
Bartender:	Once, maybe twice a week. He can't afford it. He's down on his luck.
Raymond:	Ain't everybody. He's not tipping good is he?
Bartender:	Not tonight. Like I said, he's down on his luck right now.
Raymond:	You know where he lives?
Bartender:	Not really. Just somewhere in the neighborhood.
Raymond:	Give me a Jax.

Bartender: Sure.

Bartender pulls a bottle of beer from under the bar and puts it on the counter.

                 So, what are you interested in that guy
                 for?

Raymond: We're old friends. Can't you tell?

Bartender: I noticed right off. What's his name?

Raymond: None of your damn business.

Bartender: You know, that guy looks like he's on the
                 way out.

Raymond turns to watch Celeste dance and no longer looks at the bartender during the conversation.

                 After awhile you can spot the ones that
                 can't turn the corner anymore. He seems
                 to be there.

Raymond: She don't look like Celeste.

Bartender: That's what he keeps calling her. Who's
                 that Celeste? You know?

Raymond: Just a woman.

Bartender: That's where you know him from?

Raymond: You could say that. *(drains the bottle)*

Raymond puts a fist full of bills on the bar.

This'll cover my friend's tips *(points at the stage)* and her jukebox. See you around.

Bartender: Sure.

Bartender picks the money up and starts to count it. Celeste steps down off the stage and walks over.

Celeste: Say baby. That's a hell of a wad.

Bartender: Looks like 50.

Celeste: Damn. What'd you put in his beer?

Bartender: Nothing. He's a friend of that other guy. Wanted to pay up his tips.

Celeste: Some friend.

Bartender: All night that guy was shorting me on tips. And then this. Turned out to be a pretty good night after all.

Celeste: It's dead in here, baby. When we going home?

Bartender: Same time as every night.

Celeste begins dancing by the bar. Lights fade to black.

– French Defense –

Scene II
KA BAR

Audubon Park in the New Orleans Garden District, Player is sitting on a concrete wall that runs along the edge of a pavilion. His chess computer is set up and a knapsack of his belongings sits on the ground beside him. Images in the back display oak trees and open spaces of Audbon Park. Player wears the same clothes as in the opening act except now they are wrinkled, dirty, and torn. His hair is uncombed. He constantly, aimlessly moves his hands and is unable to look directly at anyone.

Celeste sits on a park bench across from him. She is wearing sunglasses and a wide brimmed sun hat. Her look has an Audrey Hepburn style. Dr. Winter sits on the park bench beside her. Raymond stands in the shadows at the edge of the stage watching Player.

Player sets up the chess board and begins to run through the French Defense opening.

Celeste: Player?

Player turns around.

Player: Celeste?

Celeste takes off her sunglasses.

Celeste: My god you look bad.

Player: Where have you been?

Celeste: I had to take care of some business.

Player: How have you been?

French Defense – End Game

*Player won't look at her and begins moving nervously,
aimlessly shifting from position to position.*

Celeste:	Ok. We're doing ok.
Player:	That's good.
Celeste:	I shut everything down and went to Italy.
Player:	You went to Italy?
Celeste:	It seemed like a good time to leave.
Player:	Rome?
Celeste:	Milan. But we spent a few weeks in Rome.
Player:	That's good. Milan would be nice. How's Marissa?
Celeste:	She's having a good time. Sometimes she gets a little homesick. But she likes it there.
Player:	Where is she? (*he looks around for her*)
Celeste:	I have a little place in the country.
Player:	You mean you've moved to Italy?
Celeste:	For awhile.
Player:	Damn. You came out ok after all.
Celeste:	I'm lucky that way.
Player:	What are you doing now? Over there.

Celeste:	I write. Take a few classes at the university in Milan. Teach a few classes. Go to dog shows.
	You know me. I love my dogs.
Player:	Yeah, you do. How many do you have now?
Celeste:	Still two. That's about the limit for me. What about you. What have you been doing?
Player:	Nothing much lately. Things are kind of slow right now. That's the consulting game you know.

There is a long uncomfortable pause.

Celeste:	You don't look so good.
Player:	Yeah. That's what you said.
Celeste:	Still playing chess?

Celeste takes off her hat and walks across to sit on the wall by him.

Player:	I haven't been playing much lately. Today's the first time I set up the board in a long time.
Celeste:	Oh.
Player:	I got kind of burned out.
Celeste:	Baby, you were burned out before I left.
Player:	I can't snap back now.

You've been in Italy?

Celeste: Ever since Jerry was killed.

Player: Jerry's dead?

Celeste: He got it up in New York last month.

Player: He was a mad drunk.

Celeste: Yeah, he was tough.

Player: Why'd you go away?

Celeste: Business. I told you. I had a few things I had to take care of.

Player: Yeah. That's right. You've been in Italy all this time?

Celeste: Yes. It's been a while now.

Player: The cops let you leave?

Celeste: Sure. They all knew I was home that night. They figured it was a busted deal and blew it off.

Player: A busted deal.

Celeste: They all knew he was running. Jerry was such a bastard. They were all glad.

Player: What about you? You were married to him.

Celeste: They always thought he was the one running. I was just stuck with the bastard. And I always took care of the community.

Player: Still have your house in Lake Jackson?

Celeste: Yeah. Mama's living there now.

Player: That's nice. No more White Settlement huh.

Celeste: She likes it down there.

Player: Yeah. You have a nice place there.

             How'd you find me?

Celeste: You weren't that hard to find.

Celeste arranges the pieces on the board, making them centered in their squares.

Player: When you were in college he used to go to cowboy bars and get in fights. Just to fight. He was like that.

Celeste: You're in bad shape. You know that? When was the last time you had a good meal? Any meal.

Player: I remember a lot of things. He was a mad drunk. He was mad sober. I remember. I guess it all worked out for you. Why did you come back?

Celeste: To check up on you.

Player: That's what I don't get. Why would you come back here anyway. With all the cops.

Celeste:	There're no cops.
Player:	I was always a step behind the curve. Wasn't I. Always.
Celeste:	A bit.
Player:	I'm better now.
Celeste:	You haven't looked in mirror lately.
Player:	I don't have to.
Celeste:	You don't even know who I am.
Player:	Sure I do. You're my friend.
Celeste:	*(sighs)* I could always pick the losers.

Player begins moving the pieces on the chess board. Raymond steps out of the shadows.

Raymond:	Hey, freak.

Player doesn't look up and continues his aimless nervous movements. Celeste returns to sit on the park bench.

Player:	Hey, Raymond.
Raymond:	You stink, wino.
Player:	I lost my room.
Raymond:	The stink is coming out of your skin you bum.
Player:	Leave me alone, Raymond.

Raymond:	Not this time, freak.
Player:	Go away. Don't bother me.
Raymond:	You've just dropped off the edge of the world ain't you.
Player:	Why are you bothering me?
Raymond:	I'm not bothering you. I'm just talking to you. That's all. How you been doing the last couple of weeks? Hell, Spielmann thinks you got a contract off somewhere. But I knew better, you drunk. I could still smell you.
Player:	How'd you find me?

Player avoids looking at him and continues the aimless movement of his hands and head.

Raymond:	I been watching you. Sleeping over there behind the levee. Getting food out of dumpsters.
Player:	I'm just having a bit of bad luck. I'll be back.
Raymond:	You redefined bad luck. How long has it been since you had a bath?
Player:	Go away.
Raymond:	In a little while. But not yet.
Player:	What do you want? Want to play?
Raymond:	No. I'm done playing with you. I got to be moving on. Got a job down in Florida.

French Defense – End Game

Player: Whatever.

Raymond: So it's your time. Can't wait no longer.

Player: Time? What time?

Raymond: Time to settle, freak.

Raymond reaches into his jacket pocket.

Player: You don't worry me, Raymond. I had dogs that bothered me more than you.

Raymond pulls out a KA BAR knife.

Celeste: Oh my god. He's got a knife.

Player: *(suddenly coherent)* I can see that, Celeste. *(to Raymond)* What's with the KA BAR, Raymond?

Raymond: Gonna take my pound of flesh, freak.

Player: What the *hell* are you talking about?

Raymond: Killed my brother. Ran him down in the street like a dog. Left him dying in a ditch.

Player: That's a lie.

Raymond: I was there. I saw you.

Player: I never killed anybody.

Raymond: Goddamn red car going a hunert miles an hour. You never even slowed down.

Player: I never hit anybody...

Raymond: Took me a couple of months after that. But I found you. Hiding out in that freako chess club. But I waited.

Raymond grabs Player by the front of his coat and arms. They struggle but Player is too weak to break away.

Decided I wanted to see you turn to shit first. So I watched you. Every day, I sat there. Pushed you. Everyday.

You were never going to make it back to Texas. Now you got no place left to go, you piece of crap. Time to settle.

Raymond stabs him hard in the chest.

Celeste: Player!

Raymond: That's for Percy.

Raymond stabs him hard in the chest a final time. Player sags and Raymond releases him. Player remains sitting on the wall.

Raymond: That's for me and my dad.

Player: I never killed anybody.

Raymond: Saying it don't make it true, freak. You're dead, now.

Raymond wipes the blade on Players jacket, sheaths his KA BAR, and walks away. Celeste followed by Dr. Winter move to Player.

Celeste: Don't let him get away. Use the SIG. It's in your bag.

French Defense – End Game

Player: Damn it hurts. Oh God.

Celeste: Use the SIG.

Player fumbles for his bag and stops.

Player: Sorry babe.

Celeste: You're nuts. You know that?

Player: That's me.

Dr. Winter bends down and quickly examines the wounds in Player's chest.

Dr. Winter: He doesn't have long.

Dr. Winter moves back.

Celeste sits by Player, puts her arms around him, and gently rocks back and forth with him.

Celeste: Remember in *The Third Man* at the end
                   when Orson Wells was trapped. He was
                   running through the sewers tryin to get
                   away.

                   As bad as he was, selling bad penicillin
                   on the black market and all, I was hoping
                   he could get away. It didn' seem right
                   that he should be killed in a sewer.

                   Every time I watch it I hope that maybe
                   he can get away. But he never does.

Player sags into her.

                   He never does.

Dr. Winter: Celeste, he's almost gone.

Celeste: I know.

She continues to hold Player. Dr. Winter sits beside her on the concrete wall and puts the chess pieces back in their starting positions as the lights fade to black.

– French Defense –

Scene III
Coda

Paul Morphy Chess Club – the setting is the same as in the first act. MC sits in the armchair reading a chess book.

Spielmann walks in carrying his newspaper.

Spielmann: Hey MC. *(holds up his newspaper)*
                Player's dead.

Spielmann spreads the newspaper out on the center table.

                Found him stabbed to death over in
                Audubon Park last week. It's in the obits.

MC puts down his book and looks at Spielmann.

MC: Are you sure it's Player?

Spielmann: It's in the obits. Audubon Park.

MC: What the hell was he doing out there?

Spielmann: Says he was homeless.

MC: Hell.

Spielmann: I thought he was working on a contract
                down there in Texas.

MC: That's what he told me. Last I heard. Said
                he was going back to Texas for awhile.

Spielmann: I guess he didn't make it.

MC: Guess not.

Spielmann: Poor bastard. Don't know why anybody would want to kill him. He was kind of strange, but harmless.

MC: Drugs, maybe. I don't know. Did they bury him yet?

Spielmann reads the newspaper.

Spielmann: On Tuesday.

MC: The Club should have been told.

Spielmann: Says here he was a vet.

MC: He never said anything about that.

Spielmann: They buried him over at Veterans Cemetery.

You know he got the Navy Cross?

MC: No.

Spielmann: Says, his dad was an attorney in Mississippi. Looks like he'd already passed though. His mom's still living.

Had a wife. Divorced. Two kids.

Spielmann closes the newspaper.

MC: I remember him talking about the kids.

Spielmann: Yeah. We used to talk about 'em.

MC: Weren't they out in California?

Spielmann:	With his wife. Said his son was going to UCLA.
MC:	Good school.
Spielmann:	You two were about the same age?
MC:	Pretty close.
Spielmann:	I'm older than both you mugs. Air Cav in Nam. didn't get any medals though. What about you? Gulf War?
MC:	No. I never went.
Spielmann:	Yeah?
MC:	I was in the Guard but my unit didn't get deployed.
Spielmann:	Oh.
MC:	Lucky I guess.
Spielmann:	Right.
	Homeless. Man, what happened to him?
MC:	He must've been hittin' the juice.
Spielmann:	He was just in here a few weeks ago.
MC:	Maybe a couple of months ago.
Spielmann:	It wasn't that long back.
	Why didn't he tell somebody. Jeezus. If he'd asked...

MC: Asked what.

Spielmann: Asked for help.

MC: You can't turn back the clock.

Spielmann: Anybody here would have helped him.

MC: I suppose. Maybe.

Spielmann: Poor bastard. That wasn't any way to die.

MC: Because he got a Navy Cross?

Spielmann: Because he was one of us.

MC: Homeless get killed like that all the time.
                We just don't know it. That's all.

Spielmann: You know, Raymond hasn't been around
                lately either.

MC: Those two never did get a long.

Spielmann: Last time I saw him, he was talking about
                starting a group over in Florida. Tampa
                Bay area. Must've gone over there.

MC: I was hoping he'd give up that
                motorcycle thing by now.

Spielmann: Not likely. He's a main cog in that bike
                gang.

MC: Motorcycle club.

Spielmann: Yeah. It's funny how things turn out. I
                was really just stopping by to say goodby
                when I saw this article about Player.

MC: You leaving?

Spielmann: I'm moving on. I need to be closer to my
                daughter. I'm actually on my way out of
                town right now.

MC: I don't know what to say.

Spielmann holds out his hand and MC shakes it.

Spielmann: I've got to get on the road. Take care of
                that heart.

MC: You too. Don't forget to come back and
                visit sometime.

*Spielmann walks out, leaving his paper on the table. MC
watches him walk out.*

MC: Damn it's going to be quiet in here.

*MC turns around, walks to the center table, sits down and
looks at the paper.*

MC: Poor bastard.

*Bartender sticks his head in the door and looks around, sees
MC sitting at the center table and walks in.*

Bartender: Hey there. Remember me?

MC looks up.

MC: No.

Bartender: Over at the Black Cat Club a few weeks
                back. I manage the club. Fixed you the
                Left Bank?

MC: Oh, right. Good martini. What brings you over here?

Bartender: That guy you were talking to that night...

MC: You mean Player?

Bartender: Maybe, I never knew his name. But, he used to talk about this club over here all the time.

MC: Yeah. That was Player.

Bartender: So I thought I'd just come over and check it out.

MC: You play chess?

Bartender: When I was growing up.

MC: Let me get you a member's packet. We have a round robin tournament every couple of months. You'd have a lot of fun. It's a great group of people. A great group.

MC leaves the Bartender to get a membership packet.

The Bartender sits at one of the empty tables and looks around the room, studying the different details such as the tournament board.

Player and Celeste enter but he can't see them.

Player is ghost white, dressed in the clothes he was killed in, and sits at the center table. As always, Celeste carries her Bushmills and glass and sits on the arm of the stuffed chair. Player sits at one of the tables.

Celeste: What are we doing back here?

Player: I like being around the boards. Especially
                when they're empty.

                It's quiet.

Celeste: Sure it is. *(laughs long and hard)* Sure it
                is.

*MC returns with a membership packet, stops, and stares at
Player and Celeste.*

*The lights fade to black. Warren Zevon singing My Ride's
Here starts to play in the background, volume growing and
plays through to the end.*

– French Defense –

I

Problems and Choices

Chess Notation - For those who play chess, you will immediately notice that a modified old descriptive notation form is used instead of the current algebraic form of notation. This was done intentionally in the play so that the audience could more easily follow the movements taking place on the tournament board. For someone who is unfamilair with algebraic notation, saying "e4" is less meaningful than saying "Pawn to King 4." The moves being made on the board add additional tension and relevance in the performance as the names of the piece are said out loud.

Stage Direction - There is repetitive stage direction regarding the players movement and that movement of the MC character on the tournament board. This repetition is required to insure that the movements of the actors remain synchronized. Because the expected audience of the narrative is expected to be a reader, additional description was included in the stage directions to make it more readable than would otherwise be the case. In addition, direction for actors was omitted from the dialog with formatting employed to add beats to the dialog. Formating of the play was also modifed from that of a standard script to make it more readable as a narrative.

Narrative or Production - The narrative is a long three act play conceptually recast as three "movements" to allow performance on separate occasions or events. As a narrative, the three movements are intended to be read or performed in sequence.

If I were a musician, I would have written this as an opera – especially the KA BAR scene. But not a musical, something in Italian or maybe French. That would be good. An opera.

II

Background

I was introduced to the game of chess one summer while my mother was doing some extra work for the school board office. Mrs. Wardlaw was keeping my sister and me during the day and occupied us by teaching us to play chess. She and her husband were retired. He had been a railroad engineer and she had taught school. McComb, Mississippi was a railroad town where steam trains had originally stopped to refuel and change crews – long before I was born – but there were still a number of railroad jobs in town and that was a major part of what we would now call its cultural DNA.

The simple beginnings of chess for us were that the Rooks were Castles and the Knights were Horses. A couple of years later my great-uncle Adrian straightened out the terminolgy for me and routinely beat me in less than ten moves. I was not a chess prodigy. But I was captured by the game and spent hours trying to learn. My great-aunt Ivylle nicknamed me "Chess" for the few weeks one summer when I visited with them. I was nine or ten. She bought a chess set for me that Christmas. I can't describe the feeling I had when I opened the package and saw the beautiful Staunton pieces.

There were no chess computers in that age so I spent most of my time imagining chess moves and trying to think several moves ahead. That was how Uncle Adrian said chess players played.

Later, when I was in high school, I stumbled upon a book of chess openings at the local library. To me it was a book written in a foriegn language and it had a profound effect on me. I knew it was chess. I knew how to play chess. But I could not read it. Except for a brief Foreword and a few scattered annotations, it was all written in chess notation – columns of old style notation that I used (modified) in this play – with names like Nimzo Indian and French Defense. Each game and opening was identifed by the names of players (like Capablanca and Lasker) and included the year in which the game was played (like 1932 or 1927). There were no text descriptions other than a brief foreword and occasional annotation ("White has a positional advantage"). All of the contents were composed of openings and games in annotation. It was disorienting, like suddenly not being able to understand a conversation in which one had just been engaged. I read and reread the book without understanding it.

I was confused - disoriented. The certainty of reality for me was instantly changed.

Years later, when I first moved to Los Angles, I spent time visiting a chess club and even attended a regional tournament. I bought a tournament chess set and a couple of chess computers. I bought books of chess openings and tried to teach my children to play. I still buy chess programs and play. Sadly I'm not much better now than when I was in high school.

When considering a narrative vehicle that would explore individual perceptions of reality, the life of a chess player experiencing a psychotic break seemed to be a natural choice. The game is absorbing and highly internalized. Strategic decisions are complex and possible combinations of moves limitless. Thinking 10 moves ahead in a game is beyond my comprehension. It is its own reality and, for those who excel, their interior space must be vibrantly rich with patterns of thought beyond my own.

Bio

Clifford Wayne received his MFA in writing at the University of San Francisco. He is a member of the Association of Writer's and Writing Programs and the Alabama Writer's Forum. Currently he is working on his PhD at the University of South Alabama. Born in Canton, Mississippi, he grew up in LaPlace, Louisiana, but lived his adult life in Texas and California. He now resides in Alabama with his wife Theresa and two Afghan Hounds, Niki and Howl.

www.ingramcontent.com/pod-product-compliance
Lightning Source LLC
Chambersburg PA
CBHW020455100426
42813CB00031B/3369/J